County Council

Libraries, books and more . . .

Please return/renew this item by the last due date.
Library items may be renewed by phone on
030 33 33 1234 (24 hours) or via our website
www.cumbria.gov.uk/libraries

Cumbria Libraries
CLIC
Interactive Catalogue

Ask for a CLIC password

TREBLINKA

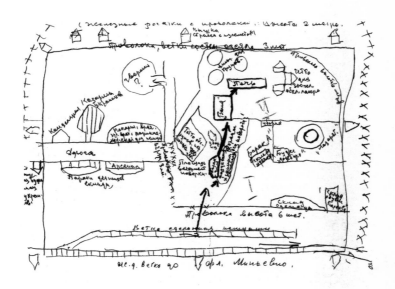

Chil Rajchman

TREBLINKA
A Survivor's Memory
1942–1943

Translated from the Yiddish by
Solon Beinfeld

MACLEHOSE PRESS
QUERCUS·LONDON

First published in Great Britain in 2011 by

MacLehose Press
an imprint of Quercus
21 Bloomsbury Square
London WC1A 2NS

For all those to whom it was not possible to tell this tale –
Andrés, Daniel, José Rajchman.

It is the writer's duty to tell the terrible truth,
and it is a reader's civic duty to learn this truth.
To turn away, to close one's eyes and walk past
is to insult the memory of those who perished.

VASILY GROSSMAN

The time had passed when each new day was bright,
precious and unique: the future stood before us,
grey and shapeless, like an impenetrable barrier.
For us, history had stopped.

PRIMO LEVI

CONTENTS

PREFACE

In mid-April 1945, American G.I.s liberated Buchenwald, while British soldiers marched, horrified, into Bergen-Belsen. There they found scenes of unimaginable suffering, men of bones and skin standing somehow on spindly legs amidst piles of emaciated corpses. Celebrated journalists documented what must have seemed the nether pole of human depravity, the worst an inhuman regime could achieve. Even as thousands of typhus-stricken survivors died, witnesses to a liberation that came too late for them, Margaret Bourke-White took chilling photographs that captured the consequences of the Nazi designs. A picture of evil was set, but Treblinka was absent from it.

Chil Rajchman's memoir of that place lay in Yiddish manuscript for decades, and the very name "Treblinka" became widely known only many years after the war's end. Yet Rajchman was witness to a very different reality, at a site the Nazis had wanted desperately to wipe from the map. It was further east, in the territories liberated by the Red Army, where far more pitiless dynamics of killing were unleashed than those that came to light at Belsen and Buchenwald. The Nazi project of extermination reached its most terrible extremity in Treblinka, and at other industrial killing centres whose names were similarly unknown.

These were places very different from the western concentration camps, which became lethal only in the last months of the war, as a failed regime lost its ability to feed its prisoners. In the eastern killing facilities, by contrast, the Nazi state did what it set out to do once it had chosen the final solution of gassing. Unlike in the west, in the east the victims were dealt immediate execution on arrival, and died as Jews targeted by the regime. Next to no-one survived: compared to the scores of memoirs testifying to the concentrations camps which, though terrible, were generally not intended to kill, only a paltry number could write of their experiences in the death camps. Just those few who, like Rajchman, were selected to operate the machinery of extermination in the *Sonderkommando* of the killing centre, and who were not put to death themselves along the way, could tell of what happened.

Rajchman's astonishing memoir – drafted mostly in hiding before the Soviets reached Warsaw, where he had fled after his unlikely survival and escape – is one of the most explicit descriptions of the Nazi project of extermination at its most spare and deadly. Indeed, the era can be known for its true horror thanks only to a handful of texts like this one.

*

In contrast to the western concentration camps, which were

established before World War II for Adolf Hitler's various internal enemies (communists and criminals were their main residents until the war, and indeed during much of it), the extermination camps of the east appeared in the heat of conflict on the eastern front. In the second half of 1941 the process of exterminating the Jews gradually shifted. Dominated immediately after Germany's invasion of the Soviet Union by mass shootings beyond the Molotov–Ribbentrop line, it now turned into a policy of constructing death factories behind it, as incursions in the east in Operation Barbarossa slowed and a lightning victory came to seem out of reach.

Following Heinrich Himmler's orders, the S.S. began by setting up Chełmno, in the Wartheland district of Greater Germany, and then Bełżec and Sobibór across the border in the "General Government", as the Nazis called their new colony made up of former Polish territories. Then Himmler ordered the erection of a new site, closer to Warsaw, also part of the General Government and its largest city. Situated some ninety kilometres northeast of the city on the Bug river, Treblinka was completed in June 1942. It became the centrepiece of "Operation Reinhard", as the project of exterminating the Jews of the General Government came to be known (in honour of Reinhard Heydrich, a lieutenant of Himmler's who had been assassinated that spring). In the end, 1.3 million Jews were killed as part of the operation – nearly 800,000 of them at Treblinka itself – in not much more than a year.

As if his destiny of living through so much death cuts him off from his previous existence, Rajchman tells nothing of his life before the "grim freight waggons" bear him to this place in the memoir's opening lines. But more information is available in testimonies he later recorded for the United States Holocaust Memorial Museum in 1988, and for the U.S.C. Shoah Foundation Institute in 1994. Born Yekhiel Meyer Rajchman – Chil for short – on 14 June, 1914, in Łódź, he fled east with a sister as the Germans invaded Poland in 1939. When the final solution began in earnest with the Soviet campaign two years later, Rajchman found himself in the vicinity of Lublin, from where he was deported to Treblinka in the round-ups intended to erase a millennial Jewish presence from the area.

Arrival at Treblinka meant the immediate loss of his sister, along with all the other women and children with whom he travelled there. The only work for which selection is possible at a death camp is for the handful of men needed to run the camp itself. Across the Molotov–Ribbentrop line, mobile killing units took on the job of extermination; at Treblinka, as at the other death facilities, the logistics of destruction called for only a few dozen S.S., some assistants (mostly Ukrainian) and the Jews themselves. Rajchman refers to his killers indiscriminately as "murderers", with only a few singled out by name or nickname, notably Kurt Franz, "the doll", notorious for his dog, his vanity and his cruelty. Rajchman knows the cremation specialist (almost certainly Herbert Floss) summoned for his expertise simply as "the artist". And in passing he mentions Ivan, dubbed "the terrible", a sadistic brute whom Rajchman later believed he recognized in Ivan Demjanjuk, and at whose American trial he testified.

*

Rajchman's memoir is above all else an incisive depiction of how the Nazis organized the destruction of millions of human beings and, indeed, reorganized it as time went on. As a worker he moves from Treblinka 1 to Treblinka 2, sections of the killing centre compartmentalized from each other by the gas chambers, to which arriving Jews are led along the *Schlauch*, the corridor the Germans euphemistically dubbed the "road to heaven". Rajchman avoids that route somehow, and observes how man-made mass death is implemented. If he knows on arrival what this place is – poignantly telling his sister not to bother taking their bags from the train – he learns the details of its "professional" evil only through harsh experience.

In brief, succeeding chapters, Rajchman tells of the infernal division of labour, through which the steps in the process of extermination are carefully apportioned, and whose shifting roles allow him to survive. He begins as a barber, shearing women's hair prior to their gassing, a fate many of them clearly foresee in one of Rajchman's most affecting passages. Transferred to the secretive, other zone of the camp, he carries bodies, asphyxiated by carbon monoxide generated from a diesel motor and often transformed beyond recognition, intertwined with one another, and repulsively swollen. Later, and for most of his time there,

Rajchman is made a so-called "dentist", part of a group of Jews charged with extracting gold from the teeth of corpses and searching the bodies for hidden valuables.

If the work evolves as Polish Jewry meets its end, it is because the Nazis seek a way to eliminate the evidence of their deeds. They order thousands of corpses dug up for burning after a policy change alters the method of disposal from burial to cremation. In the early days, the Jews are told to layer sand carefully over the tombs, but – as if in a sickening act of posthumous resistance – the blood of the Jews is "unable to rest", and "thrust[s] itself upwards to the surface". After an era of crude and unsuccessful bonfires, the "artist" arrives and teaches them how to do it. The task is massive, as the formerly interred corpses have to be aflame along with newly killed bodies, hundreds of thousands of them per month for a time. Women burn more easily; placed at the base, they are the torches that will consume the rest. But there are still fragments of bones that the Nazis force the Jews to collect, painstakingly, often thwarting their hopes of leaving some trace – anything – to be discovered of this infamy.

Inside the camp, a tenuous solidarity rules, even as the unbearable circumstances push many *Sonderkommando* members to suicide. For others, plans for escape germinate, leading eventually to the extraordinary insurrection of 2 August, 1943. From the day Rajchman arrives at Treblinka to the fateful day he revolts and escapes, physical depredations are omnipresent. Hunger is constant, and illness a frightening threat. The beatings and whippings Rajchman and others repeatedly suffer are understood to be dangerous on account of their potential consequences. A wounded face means certain death. Injury is repaid by execution, and Rajchman is fortunate that a fellow Jew can treat his suppurating cut with impromptu surgery. Throughout, the prose of this memoir is factual, and all the more devastating for its exquisitely controlled rage at the crimes he is describing. By the end, his anger has already crystallized in resistance and flight for the sake of life and memory.

*

Would it have made a difference had Rajchman's memories come to light immediately after the events they describe? Perhaps not. Yankel Wiernik, whom Rajchman mentions, published his story of a year in Treblinka in Polish in 1944; it was translated into a number of other languages thereafter, but did not attract much attention. Other memoirists, notably Richard Glazar and Shmuel Willenberg, eventually published their testimonies. Their grim tasks mostly accomplished, the death camps – including Treblinka – were razed; only Majdanek, which like Auschwitz combined labour and extermination, survived long enough to be liberated by the Soviets, who publicized their findings as assaults on humanity. The brilliant Soviet-Jewish writer Vasily Grossman visited Treblinka after the arrival of the Red Army in summer 1944, and on the basis of few sources drafted and published that same autumn an exceptionally powerful description of the camp. Reproduced in this volume as a complement to Rajchman's memoir, Grossman's report is a masterpiece of investigation, a damning indictment of the inhumanity that he knew had occurred, no matter how fervently the Nazis had hoped they could suppress all evidence of it as they departed. Given the scattering of Treblinka's tiny number of survivors, Grossman's extraordinary reconstruction showed how difficult it would be to gain reliable information about the site – but also that it would be possible to grasp this nether pole of human evil.

The Soviets who conquered these lands were therefore better positioned than Westerners to grasp the true nature of the death camps. Yet the disproportionate victimhood of Jews was not ideologically useful from the perspective of Moscow, or in the other capitals of Eastern Europe where the Red Army finally defeated Hitler. From the perspective of official antifascism, "humanity" had suffered, not one group within it more than the rest. In 1944 Grossman clearly registered the Jewish identity of Treblinka's victims, but he did not emphasize it. A number of survivors, including Rajchman, testified before a post-war Polish historical commission, and soon afterwards Rachel Auerbach synthesized in Yiddish what was known. (Auerbach later became a leading figure at Israel's Yad Vashem memorial.) Yet a year later, when Grossman, in collaboration with Ilya Ehrenburg, finished a *Black Book* detailing Nazi crimes against Jews and sought to reincorporate his Treblinka essay, the Soviets could not accept that the victims had been predominantly Jewish. Though Grossman's essay had already been circulated elsewhere (and had been translated into a number of languages), the plates of the *Black Book* were destroyed. Whether in the west, where Belsen and Buchenwald were so prominent, or in the east, no-one else could allow themselves to see what Rajchman and his fellow survivors of the Treblinka revolt did.

Having been constructed as a concentration camp in 1940, Auschwitz, to the west of the General Government, surged as a death facility after Treblinka had done its work. Those who were killed there were mainly Jews and others from beyond Poland, including Hungarian Jewry in a paroxysm in 1944, but because many sorts of people were interned there, and many Jews as workers, its survivors were by an enormous measure witness to a western-style internment rather than an eastern-style death factory. Many of its more than 100,000 survivors (a large number of whom were not Jews) presented Auschwitz as a concentration camp in immediate Soviet publicity, and even at the Nuremberg trials. The atrocities that took place at its Birkenau site – a death facility like Treblinka, but confusingly embedded in a universe of internment and labour – were neglected for a long time. The death camps became known only later, as the wheels of justice began to grind, and Holocaust memory coalesced decades after the fact.

*

Rajchman's escape leads only to new travails. There is a moving portrait of flight through the countryside, in which human kindness and the unconscionable collaboration of local Polish peasants are both evident. He barely mentions it, but Rajchman lived through the 1944 Warsaw uprising against the Nazis, and ultimately – after the Soviet liberation of the city in January 1945 – migrated to Uruguay, where he lived a productive life in the business world and had three sons. It appears that some additions were made to this crucial documentation after the war (certainly the final few paragraphs), and some other revisions may have taken place. A friend of Rajchman's family then agitated for its publication. As fate would have it, this work is posthumous: Rajchman died in 2004.

That Rajchman bore witness to Treblinka's horrors, that his memoir has belatedly appeared, is a gift, but one which is bleak and discomfiting, not redemptive and uplifting. Even the Treblinka revolt, often treated as an uncomplicated triumph of the human spirit, is narrated by this participant in tones that are far from straightforwardly heroic. Rajchman bore witness, but he did not offer lessons: the memoir's insights seem to be for a posterity that still does not know how to respond to this past.

Through the unprecedented landscape of his text, Rajchman's proofs of how far beyond the boundaries of the imaginable humans can go in their treatment of one another are piled more obscenely than the mountains of corpses the Nazis put to the torch. In the end, the list of abominations seems to offer too many faces of evil for its readers to decide what was most atrocious in this place and time.

But my choice, I think, is Rajchman's disturbing reflection – offered in passing, but all the more upsetting for that reason – that it was better for him to lose his mother when he was a child than for her to live long enough to descend into a hell she would never have escaped. It is a dismal testament to their destruction of the ordinary moral world that the Nazis could make one of the worst imaginable events of any life seem like it had been a fortunate event.

SAMUEL MOYN

TREBLINKA

I

In sealed railway freight waggons to an unknown destination.

The grim freight waggons transport me there, to that place. They are transporting from all directions: from east and west, from north and south. By day and by night. In all seasons of the year people are brought there: spring and summer, autumn and winter. The transports travel there without hindrance and without limit, and Treblinka grows richer in blood day by day. The more people who are brought there, the more Treblinka is able to receive them.

I, like all the others, do not know where and for what reason we are travelling. Nevertheless we try, insofar as possible, to find out something about our journey. The Ukrainian robbers who guard us will not do us the favour of replying. The only thing we hear from them is: – Hand over gold, hand over money and valuables! These criminals visit us constantly. Almost every hour another one of them terrorizes us. They beat us mercilessly with their rifle butts, and each of us tries as best he can to shut the murderers up with a few zlotys in order to avoid their blows. That is what our journey is like.

We travel from Lubartów station, some 20 kilometres from Lublin. I travel with my pretty young sister Rivka, nineteen years old, and a good friend of mine, Wolf Ber Rojzman, and his wife and two children. Almost all those in the freight waggon are my close acquaintances, from the same small town, Ostrów Lubelski. There are about 140 of us in the freight waggon. It is extraordinarily tight, with dense, stale air, all of us pressed against one another. Despite the fact that men and women are all together, each of us, in these crowded conditions, has to perform his natural functions on the spot where he is standing . . . One hears groans from all four corners, and people asking each other: – Where are we going? Everyone shrugs and replies with a deep oy. No-one knows where the road leads, and at the same time no-one wants to believe that we are going where our sisters and brothers, our nearest and dearest, have been sent over a period of many months.

Sitting near me is my friend Katz, an engineer by profession. He assures me that we are going to Ukraine and that we will be able to settle in the countryside there and work the land. He explains that he knows this for certain because that is what he was told by a German lieutenant, the manager of a state farm in Jedlanka, 7 kilometres from our little town. The German told Katz this ostensibly as a friend, since Katz had from time to time repaired an electric motor for him. I want to believe it, though I know it is in fact not so.

We travel. The train stops often because of the signals, since it is running outside the timetable and therefore has to wait and let the normal trains through. We travel through various stations, among them Luków and Siedlce. At every opportunity, when the train stops, I beg the Ukrainians, who descend to the platform, to bring us a little water. They do not reply, but if you give them a gold watch, they hand you a sip of water. Many of my friends give them their valuables but do not receive the promised water. I am an exception. I ask a Ukrainian for a little water. He demands 100 zlotys from me for a bottle of water. I agree. In a short while he brings me a half-litre bottle of water. I ask him how long we will be travelling. His reply is: – Three days, because we are going to Ukraine. I begin to think maybe it's really true . . . We have been travelling for nearly fifteen hours, though the distance is about 120 kilometres.

It is 4.00 in the morning as we approach a station called Treblinka, which lies some 7 kilometres from Małkinia. We stop. The cars are sealed and we don't know what will happen to us. We wait for the train to move again. My sister tells me she is hungry. But we have little in the way of food. Leaving our town unexpectedly, it was impossible to procure supplies. The same was true in the town of Lubartów. I explain to my sister that we still have a long way to go and we have to restrict our eating as much as possible, or our food won't last the journey. She agrees, assuring me that she really isn't so hungry after all.

2

We enter a forest. Treblinka. Before our eyes – an image of death.
Men to the right, women to the left!

After a short while, the train begins to move. By now it is light outside. We become uneasy because we see that the train is moving backwards. The train moves slowly and we enter a forest. We look at each other uncertainly. The answer is: who knows? But soon there appears before our eyes a grim and terrible scene. A scene of – death. Through a small opening I see great piles of clothes. I realize that we are lost. Alas, it is hopeless. After a short while the door of the freight waggon is abruptly thrown open to the accompaniment of fiendish screams: – *Raus! Raus!* (Get out! Get out!) I no longer have any doubts about our misfortune. I take my sister by the arm and try to get out of the freight waggon as quickly as possible. I leave everything in the freight waggon. My poor sister asks me why I am leaving our baggage behind. I reply: – We won't be needing it . . . I don't manage to say even a few more words to her before we hear a murderous shout: – Men to the right, women to the left! I barely have time to kiss her and we are torn apart for ever.

Blows begin raining down on us from all sides. The murderers drive us in rows into an open space and scream at us to surrender our gold, money and valuables immediately. Anyone who tries to conceal anything will be shot. Nearly all of us part with what we still have. Then we are ordered to undress quickly and tie our shoes together by the laces. Everyone undresses as quickly as possible, because the whips are flying over our heads. Whoever undresses a bit more slowly is savagely beaten.

Treblinka is built in a professional way. On arrival it might appear to be an ordinary train station. The platform is long and wide enough to accommodate a normal train of as many as forty cars. A few dozen metres from the platform two barracks stand facing one another. In one, on the right, is stored the food that people bring with them. The barracks on the left is where the women and children undress. The murderers are so considerate that they do not require the women to undress in the open air along with the men. On the way to their deaths, from which there is no return, men and women will meet intimately.

To the left of the platform stand several wooden structures, among them the kitchen and the workshops. Opposite these are the sleeping quarters. Nearby are the barracks where the S.S. men live. The S.S. barracks are provided with every comfort. To the right of the railway platform there is a big space where clothes, shoes, underwear, bedclothes and other things are gathered. Here several hundred workers sort the clothing and carry it to a special place. Every few days the sorted clothing is sent to Germany on lorries.

Opposite the platform where the barracks stand begins the road to the gas chambers, known as the *Schlauch* (feeder tube). The road is planted with small trees and looks like a garden path. Down this road, which is covered with a layer of white sand, all must run naked. No-one returns from this road. People driven down this road are beaten mercilessly and stabbed with bayonets, so that after they have been driven down it, the road is covered in blood.

A special commando, known as the *Schlauch-Kolonne*, cleans the road after every transport. They spread fresh sand so that the next victims will be unaware.

The *Schlauch* road is not long. In a few minutes you find yourself in a white structure, on which a Star of David is painted. On the steps of the structure stands a German, who points to the entrance and smiles: – *Bitte, bitte!* The steps lead to a corridor lined with flowers and with long towels hanging on the walls.

The size of the gas chamber is 7 by 7 metres. In the middle of the chamber there are shower-heads through which the gas is introduced. On one of the walls a thick pipe serves as an exhaust to remove the air. Thick felt around the doors of the chamber renders them airtight.

In this building there are some ten gas chambers. At a short distance from the main structure there is a smaller one with three gas chambers. By the doors stand several Germans who shove people inside. Their hands do not rest for a moment as they scream fiendishly: – Faster, faster, keep moving!

I am already undressed and look around. I no longer have any doubts about our fate. We are helpless. I notice that in the barracks opposite us, the women and children are undressing, and we can hear their pitiful screams. It is impossible to get near them. We are ordered to line up in rows. We stand as we are ordered to. Those who are still undressing are beaten mercilessly. When nearly all of us are lined up, the guards approach and choose some hundred men, only young ones, and have us stand aside. The others are led away. Where, no-one knows. I find myself among the chosen hundred young men. From a distance, I see my friend Rojzman with his son, and, not really knowing whether it is better for him, I gesture to him to run over to me in my group.

We stand for a few minutes until all the other men have been led away, and then we are led back to the baggage that the Jews brought with them. Each of us must grab a bundle bigger than himself; if anyone takes a smaller bundle he is whipped repeatedly. We are driven to a big space. Along the way guards are posted, arms linked in a human chain, so that no-one will escape the whips.

I am astounded by the terrible scene: you see several

mountains of piled-up parcels. We are driven to one such stack where parcels of bedclothes and sacks are lying. People stand by the stack sorting the contents. I see that they are all Jews and, running past, try to ask them: – Brothers, tell me, what is this? Unfortunately I receive no reply. Each of them tries to turn his head away so as not to have to answer. I ask them again: – Tell me, what is going on here? One of them replies: – Brother, do not ask. We are lost!

The running back and forth with the bundles happens so fast that I no longer know what is happening to me. We make several round trips, the bundles are cleared away, and we are driven back to our own piles of clothes. We are ordered to retrieve the pairs of shoes which each of us had tied by the laces. We grab the shoes and are driven back to the big open space to a second stack, which is about four storeys high and which consists of nothing but shoes, tens of thousands of pairs of shoes. After the shoes, the clothes that we men had taken off are cleared away. We change direction to another stack which consists only of clothes. After the space is finally cleared, we are driven into the barracks where the women undressed. Before my eyes lie the clothes of the poor women, among them those of my pretty young sister. I look around, but none of the women are there. They have all been led away, driven further on. I am distracted for a moment, pick up a small bundle and try to move forward. I am hit so hard with a wire whip that I nearly black out. The murderer screams at me like a stuck pig: – You dog, the bundle is too small!

I hardly know what is happening to me. I throw myself to the ground, spread my arms as wide as possible and grab as much as I can. I run out quickly, because the last ones remaining are beaten mercilessly.

We run back and forth several times with the bundles with the whips falling on us every step of the way.

3

I am chosen as a barber.

I sort clothing until the next transports arrive. Once, when I straighten up, I am beaten till I bleed.

I no longer know where I am in the world. Suddenly, running back for more bundles, I hear one of the murderers, an S.S. man, shout: – Which of you is a barber?

I look around and see that four undressed men are already standing to one side, among them my friend Leybl Goldfarb from our town. I run over to them and announce that I am a barber.

The murderer asks me if I am telling the truth. I answer: – *Jawohl!* He tells me to go over to the four others – I am the fifth. Several others try to run over after me, but he does not want to take any more. The answer is: – *Es reicht* (That's enough).

He orders us to come with him immediately to the storeroom where the sorted men's clothes are lying. He orders the Jews working there to give us something to put on, and each of us quickly receives a pair of trousers and a jacket. I ask for a shirt, but the Jew who works there tells me to be quiet and dress as quickly as possible. He says to me: – Brother, you have been saved from death! I quickly put on the trousers and jacket. The other four Jews do the same.

The murderer leads me to another place and orders that we be given shoes. Each of us grabs a pair of shoes and quickly puts them on. We are then led to another place where Jews are sorting parcels and are ordered to stay there and sort. When a new transport arrives we are to be released, since we are intended for barbering.

I have no notion of barbering and no idea what will happen if I cannot do the work. But I tell myself that after all it cannot be worse than dying . . .

As I stand among the piles to be sorted, I notice other men from my transport running past, and suddenly I see my friend Rojzman among them. I yell to him to run over to the German who took me from the other place and tell him that he is a barber too. Rojzman runs over to the German and the answer is a whip over his head. Alas, that is the last time I see my friend. He is driven away for ever.

We are at once put to work sorting. My friend Leybl stands next to me. We inspect every garment as carefully as possible. On the other side of me stands a worker who has already been here for several days. I want to find out from him what happens here, since, despite the fact that I see the clothes left behind by the victims, I still cannot grasp what is going on. He advises me: – Remember, don't talk, try to stay bent over, don't straighten up or you will feel the whip.

I bend over more deeply and ask him again what happens here.

– Don't you see? Here they take the lives of our nearest and dearest. Don't you see that these are the clothes of the poor wretches who come here?

He is afraid to talk too much. The fear here is tremendously strong. I tell him that the five of us were selected from the transport as barbers and I don't know what our work will be. I find out that he too belongs to the barbers, and that our work consists of cutting off the hair of all the women. I want to find out from him how the work is done and he answers: – You'll see.

I leave him alone and continue to sort the clothes, one by one, just like the others. I look around and see a lot of suitcases. Each suitcase contains something different. For example, the main suitcase is for money. It quickly fills up with gold, money and valuables. From time to time a special worker, called the Gold-Jude, comes around and carries away the filled suitcases. Then there are suitcases for small valuables like watches, others for razors, cigarette lighters and various other things. Everything has to be sorted separately.

My neighbour urges me to select a good, sharp pair of scissors for my work. I find a pair of barber shears and tell my friend Leybl to do the same, since he knows about as much about barbering as I do.

The clock strikes 12.00 and we hear a bugle call. Everyone heads in the direction of the place where we are to be given a midday meal. My friend and I try to stay close to our neighbour, since we don't yet know how things are done here. Everyone tries to get as close to the kitchen as possible. We all stand in rows of five. After a short while we move in the direction of the kitchen. When we come to the kitchen, the window is still closed. We wait for several minutes, then, marching in groups of five past the little window, we get the soup. Everyone tries to eat as quickly as possible. Soon we hear the bugle call again. All of us have to stand in rows as before. That has to happen very quickly: whoever gets disorientated and doesn't stand in the right place is whipped.

I continue to stay close to my neighbour. With a few minutes to spare, I try to learn from him how to go about the work. His explanation is as follows: when a fresh transport arrives, the same murderer rushes over. His name is Kiewe; he has been here a long time. He yells out: – Barbers! and we have to report at once. We are led to the chamber where our brothers and sisters are gassed. My neighbour points out that we have to cut the hair as quickly as possible. It must all happen extraordinarily fast. The murderers are standing around and whoever cuts slowly is badly beaten.

The bugle call sounds again and we get ready. Each group is inspected and then we move, each to his place. The work continues. I try to go through the clothing as quickly as possible, but

I forget that it is forbidden to stand upright. I straighten up for a few minutes and suddenly one of the bandits approaches and starts to whip me without stopping. Then he asks me if I know why I was whipped. I answer: – *Jawohl!* The bandit has cut me in the head and blood runs over my face. I find a bottle of water and put a wet rag to my head. My neighbour yells: – Remember to stay bent over, or you'll get more lashes!

I bend over. With one hand I hold the wet rag to my head, and with the other I sort the clothes. It is a long time before I stop bleeding. My face is bloody, and my friend quietly tells me to wash it, because anyone with the marks of blows on his face is shot.

I try to wash myself and get back to work. After a while, my foreman orders me to take the sorted bundles to the warehouse. He shows me the way and warns me to make it fast, especially on the way back, when I am not carrying anything. I grab a parcel and head in the direction of the storage area for men's coats. I put down my load and see that every few metres there is a great pile of various kinds of clothing and every pile has a sign indicating what is in it.

I hurry back to my work, and by carrying the bundles I become familiar with the place and know where everything is located. The work goes much too quickly. Every few minutes the murderers come with whips in their hands and shout: – Faster. Get moving!

From time to time they order the workers to lie down and give them a few hard lashes. After the blows you have to get up quickly and run back to work. That is what our work is like.

4

First night in the barracks. Moyshe Ettinger tells how he saved
himself and cannot forgive himself. The evening prayer
is recited and Kaddish is said for the dead.

It is 6.oo in the evening. We hear a bugle call. We stop work and stand to attention in groups of five. The foreman, a Jewish engineer called Galewski, counts us and makes his report. We hear an orchestra playing. We turn right and move in the direction of the kitchen. The kitchen window is opened and we approach it in rows to get our soup. We head for the barracks, which stand opposite the kitchen. The barracks are filled to capacity and we have to lie on the ground.

I look at my friend Leybl and he at me and our tears pour down like rain. Each of us asks the other why he is crying. I cannot answer. I have lost the power of speech. We try to comfort and calm one another as much as possible. Leybl, I say to him,

yesterday at this time my young sister was still alive. He answers: –
And my whole family, my brothers and twelve thousand poor Jews
from my town.

And yet we are alive and witness this great misfortune and are
so hardened that we can eat and endure the heartbreak. How can
one be so strong, have such unnatural strength to endure? As we
stand there, we notice a friend, Moyshe Ettinger, from our town.
He falls on us sobbing. After he has calmed down a bit, he tells us
that yesterday he was running naked to the gas chamber. Along
the way he happened upon a pile of clothing and crawled into the
middle of it. He grabbed a pair of trousers and a jacket from the
pile and put them on. Not far away he saw a Jew marching past.
He begged him to save him and find him a pair of shoes. Fortunately, the worker found a pair and brought them to him. Then he
worked his way out of his hiding place and stood near the pile of
clothing and began sorting it. The workers standing next to him
helped him and told him what to do. In that way he saved himself
from death.

Now he stands next to us and weeps. He cannot forgive
himself for having saved himself when his wife and child went to
their deaths. We are all as if drugged. Yesterday all of my family
were living and now – all are dead. Each of us stands as if turned
to stone. I weep for my fate, for what I have lived to see.

At that moment I hear, to the left of the barracks, the miserable
survivors standing and saying the evening prayers, and after
praying they recite Kaddish for the dead with tears in their eyes.

Kaddish wakes me up. I look closely: yes, all who are here are wretched orphans and accursed individuals. I become almost wild and shout at them: – To whom are you reciting Kaddish? You still believe? In what do you believe, whom are you thanking? Are you thanking the Lord for his mercy in taking away our brothers and sisters, our fathers and mothers? No, no! It is not true; there is no God. If there were a God, he would not allow such misfortune, such transgression, where innocent small children, only just born, are killed, where people who want only to do honest work and make themselves useful to the world are killed! And you, living witnesses of the great misfortune, remain thankful. Whom are you thanking?

My grief-stricken friend Leybl tries to settle me: – Calm yourself, you're right. Yesterday all my brothers and sisters and their little ones were alive, and today they are no longer in this world.

He is trying to calm me, he is beside himself and begs me: – Yekhiel, don't shout, you know where we are . . .

He is shouting louder than I am.

We fall to the ground from fatigue and cannot get up. I lie there and remind myself that I wronged my poor sister. A few minutes before she died I dissuaded her from eating a piece of bread so she was driven hungry to her death. Did she forgive me? The murderers have robbed all of us of our understanding.

We lie like that in our pain. The clock strikes 9.00 in the evening. The barracks are locked, the lights turned off. I lie on the ground all night.

5

I work as a barber. My sister's dress. The last wish of an old Jewish woman. The laughter of an eighteen-year-old girl . . . We sing a song.

At 5.00 in the morning we are awakened by the alarm and we tear ourselves from our sleep. We walk to the kitchen. Each of us receives coffee and bread, and at 6.00 – off to work. I discover that there are several groups of sorters. Each group takes its place separately, and after all of them are counted, some seven hundred people in total, each group is led away to work with its *Kapo* and foreman at the head. I am given the same work as the day before, sorting clothes. While sorting I find the dress that my sister was wearing. I stop, grasp the dress, hold it for a moment and examine it from every angle. I show it to my neighbour. He drops his guard for a moment and pities me. Then immediately he shouts: – You are forgetting yourself. Naturally; who can help himself? Our fate is so wretched. But remember, you can get the whip for that.

I tear off a piece of the dress and hide it in my pocket. (I had that piece of the dress with me for ten months, the whole time I was in Treblinka.)

The clock strikes 8.oo. The foreman suddenly calls out: – Barbers!

All the barbers, ten men, five old and five new ones, stand next to him. He asks if each of us has shears (we have all provided ourselves with a pair) and then leads us away to the evil gas chambers, where the living are transformed into the dead.

He leads us into the first cell, which is open to the corridor and to the outside. It is a fine summer's day. The sun's rays reach us. Long benches are set out and next to them dozens of suitcases.

The murderer orders us to take our places. Each of us stands behind a suitcase. A band of Ukrainians surrounds us, whips in their hands and rifles on their shoulders. The *Kommandant* of Treblinka comes in – a tall, stout murderer of about fifty. He orders us to work fast. After five cuts the hair must be all cut off. We have to make sure that no hair falls on the ground, and the suitcases must be fully packed. He ends his order this way: – If not, you will be whipped, you accursed dogs!

We stand as if paralyzed. A few minutes pass and we hear pitiful screams. Naked women appear. In the corridor stands a murderer who tells them to run into the room where we are. They are beaten murderously and driven with cries of "Faster, faster!"

I stare wide-eyed at the victims and cannot believe my eyes. Each woman sits down opposite a barber. A young woman sits down opposite me. My hands are paralyzed and I cannot move my fingers. The women sit opposite us and wait for us to cut off their beautiful hair, and their weeping is pitiful and terrible.

My friend next to me shouts: – Remember, you will be lost, because a murderer is standing there and can see you working slowly!

I force open the fingers of my dirty hand, cut off the woman's hair and throw it into the suitcase like every one of us is doing. The woman stands up. I see that she is dazed from the blows she has received. She asks me where to go and I indicate the second entryway, on the left. Before I have time to turn around, a second woman is already sitting down. She takes my hand and wants to kiss me: – I beg you, tell me, what do they do with us? Is this already the end?

She weeps and begs me to tell her if it is a difficult death, if it takes long, if people are gassed or electrocuted . . .

I do not reply. She will not leave me alone and begs me to tell her, because she knows that in any case she is lost. Nevertheless I cannot tell the truth and calm her. The whole conversation lasts a few seconds, as long as it takes me to cut her hair. I turn away because I cannot look her in the eye. The murderer standing near us shouts: –

Los! Schneller die Haare schneiden! (Come on! Cut the hair faster!) The woman is bewildered. After a bit she jumps up and runs out.

One victim after the other sits down and the shears cut and cut the hair without stopping. Weeping and screaming can be heard. Many women tear off pieces of their own living flesh and we have to look on and are forbidden to say anything.

An elderly woman sits down in front of me. I cut her hair and she begs me to grant her a last wish before her death: to cut her hair a bit more slowly, because after her, opposite my friend, stands her young daughter, and she wants them to go to their deaths together. I try to oblige the woman and at the same time I ask my friend to speed up his cutting. I want to fulfill the last request of the elderly woman. But unfortunately the murderer screams at me and whips my head. I have to hurry and cannot help the woman any more. She has to run without her daughter . . .

Continuing to cut hair, I suddenly hear a shout. I turn and see a young girl of about eighteen run inside and begin shouting at all the women: – What is the matter with you? You ought to be ashamed! For whom are you crying? You should be laughing! Let our enemies see that we do not go to our deaths as cowards. The murderers enjoy our weeping!

All stand as if frozen to the spot. The murderers look around. They become even wilder and the girl laughs in their faces until she leaves.

From among the wretched victims a pretty young girl sits down in front of me. She begs me: – Do not cut off all my hair. What will I look like?

I cannot reply. What can I say to her? I try to calm her . . .

A woman sits before me. She tears out her hairpins and shouts at me: – Faster! Do what you want. You can even cut some of the flesh out of my scalp. I know that I am lost . . .

Yes, we are all lost.

An older woman begs me to tell her if all the men are kept alive as labourers. She knows that she is going to her death. Still, she will be happy if her son, who came with her, remains alive. I calm her with my answer and she thanks me. She is content that her son will remain alive and take revenge on the murderers . . .

Thus hundreds of women pass through with weeping and shouting and I have become an automaton that cuts off their hair.

Suddenly the shoving of the next group of victims is interrupted because the gas chambers are over-full. The murderer standing by the door of the cell announces that there will be a break of half an hour and goes away. Some Ukrainians and several S.S. men remain with us. I look around and think: Good God, what kind of hell is this? The murderers force us to cut off the hair of our sisters a few minutes before their deaths and we, temporarily spared, do it in the shadow of the whips. We have been deprived of our reason and are the tools of criminals. My friend who worked with me sorting clothes asks me quietly: – Why have you changed so much? I don't recognize you!

I don't reply and he leaves me alone.

It doesn't take long, and several murderers come in and order us to sing a song. But only a beautiful song.

The old barbers already know what that means: if we don't

sing, we will be beaten mercilessly, and out of fear several begin to sing. I am as if paralyzed: over there in the chamber they gas people and we are supposed to sing! A murderer, noticing that my mouth is closed, screams at me: – You dog, do you want to get it on your mug?

I open my mouth as if I were singing. Alas, we have to sing and amuse the murderers.

From time to time one of them goes out into the corridor and looks through a small window to ascertain if the victims are dead.

Half an hour passes in this way. A murderer comes in and announces that work is resuming. We must once again take our places in order to receive new victims. Once again we hear pitiful cries and soon naked women appear.

The work proceeds without hindrance. The whole transport is disposed of in an hour: several thousand people have been gassed.

6

New transports. To the gas chambers with "Shema Yisroel".
Our first decision to escape. My last days in Camp 1.

The work is finished. Our section chief comes in and announces that the transport has been liquidated. We close the suitcases and place them to one side. We are immediately escorted to the open space and in the shadow of the dreaded whips we must forget that we have cut the hair of thousands of women. Now once again we have to search for money, gold and valuables for the murderers and again sort clothes. The chief notifies our foreman, Scher from Częstochowa, that by 12.00 the pile of *Scheisse* (shit) must be cleared away. From time to time S.S. men come to the square and order us to pick out good-quality suits and watches for them and fine dresses for their wives. We must hurry for the pile must at all costs be cleared away by noon.

The clock strikes 12.00. We are already standing by the kitchen when we hear the locomotive entering the camp again, dragging fresh victims with it. The same freight waggons appear and we hear the doors thrown open quickly, and as always everyone is driven out of the waggons with blows from rifle butts and whips. A few minutes later the head murderer of the camp appears and shouts: – Barbers, step out! We have not yet eaten our midday soup but are at once led back to the gas chambers, to more of our filthy work. And the same terrifying picture: more wretched souls appear, from the town of Ostrowice. In just over an hour it is all over for them.

Before me sits a young woman. I cut her hair and she grabs my hand and begs me to remember that I too am a Jew. She knows that she is lost. But remember, she says, you see what is being done to us. That's why my wish for you is that you will survive and take revenge for our innocent blood, which will continue to cry out . . .

I reply quietly: – My dear woman, the same fate awaits me. I am a Jew, after all.

The woman has not had time to get up when a murderer walking between the benches lashes her head with his whip. Blood shows on her shorn head. She jumps up and runs where all are running.

We finish our work and remain standing at our places for a while, because the way out is filled with naked men being driven to the gas chambers. They run through a chain of murderers who stand on both sides and beat them. The Jews run with their hands raised, fingers spread wide, chanting continuously: – *Shema Yisroel, Shema Yisroel* (Hear, O Israel). With these words on their lips they are driven to their deaths.

The stream of victims comes to an end, the iron door is hermetically shut, and the last cries of the victims are silenced. The murderers appear and we are led back to the square, because the noon break is over. We sort clothes at a rapid pace in order to make room for new bundles. I sort then carry the bundles in various directions.

That is how the afternoon passes. The clock strikes 6.00. Hearing the signal, we stop working and take our places for roll-call. After counting us, the Jewish head *Kapo*, Galewski, announces the number of prisoners to the chief killer, Kiewe. He then orders: – *Rechts um!* (Right face!) in the direction of the kitchen.

As we did yesterday, each of us receives his soup and heads for the barracks. I stand with my friend Leybl and Moyshe Ettinger and the tears pour out of us without stopping. We are finally beginning to understand the catastrophe taking place here, that this is a factory that swallows victims without stopping: yesterday twelve thousand, today fifteen thousand, and so on without end . . . We want to find out what is done with the victims after they are dead, but we are unable to, because there, where the corpses are, is Camp 2, which is entirely isolated from us, and we have no contact with the Jews who work there.

We ponder and ponder and ask ourselves: What now? And we decide that at all costs we must look for possibilities to escape, because at some point, without warning, we are in any case going to be killed.

We decide that, starting tomorrow, each of us will begin to collect as much money as he can from what we find while working, trying in the next few days to collect tens of thousands of zlotys, and at the same time we will try to find a way to escape.

Meanwhile the clock strikes 9.00. The lights are turned off. Exhausted and depressed, we throw ourselves to the ground. We groan for a time with the heavy pain in our hearts, then fall asleep.

We sleep through the night and at 4.30 we hear the signal. We awake from our deep sleep. I ask around to see if I can obtain a little water to wash myself with. My friend tells me that he hasn't washed in the ten days since he came here. We march out to our breakfast of coffee and bread. I am able to save a little water to wash with. We march to the roll-call, and, after being counted, we are led by our *Kapo* and foreman to the square for work.

My friend Leybl and I get to work. When we find larger banknotes we try to hide them so that no murderer will notice, otherwise we will get a bullet in the head. We collect the money carefully and hide it in the coat I am wearing. I work that way for a couple of hours and gather several thousand zlotys. By noon I have about five thousand. My friend Leybl has somewhat more. At the noon break we decide to collect as much money as we can, since without money we are lost even if we succeed in escaping.

In the afternoon the work goes quickly. I once again find several thousand zlotys. It is about 2.00 in the afternoon. While sorting I hear, not far from me, a murderer call: – *Komm' her!* (Come here!) I drop what I am doing and run over to him. He tells me to remain standing there. There are soon about twenty of us standing together and we do not know what will happen to us. I see that more and more workers are being sent over. Fearing that we may be searched, I take off the coat in which the money is hidden. I throw it to one side saying that I'm hot. After a few minutes I and about thirty others are led to the courtyard where we all undress and are carefully searched to see if any of us has hidden money or valuables. The murderers find one man with money. He is brutally beaten, taken aside and shot.

As I am one of the last to be inspected, I am able to search my pockets and find a 100-zloty banknote. I do not become flustered and put the banknote quickly into my mouth. The murderers do not notice. They take away our pocket knives and razor blades. They line us up in groups of five and lead us towards where the victims are driven to the gas chambers. But instead of the gas chambers, we are led to the second camp, which is far worse than the gas chambers.

7

Treblinka – Camp 2. I become a carrier of corpses. Gold teeth are extracted from the dead. The technique of carrying corpses.

No sooner do we cross the threshold of the wretched camp than we are greeted with a hail of lashes from the whips, which fall unceasingly upon us. We are immediately driven to a job that consists of taking sand in barrows from one pile and carrying it to another pile. In the first minutes I think I am going to pass out. I don't know what I am carrying and where I am carrying it. Nevertheless, after running several times to the pile where we pour out the sand, I see that we are pouring it onto corpses that have been thrown into a pit. I am unable to gather my thoughts because they do not let us rest for a second. We load the sand with the greatest possible speed, grab the barrow immediately and run, dump the sand onto the victims and then run back again. The sweat is pouring off our faces. I throw off my jacket, but that doesn't help. At every step there stand the murderers who lash every one of our heads with their long whips. I expend my last ounce of strength and am no longer able to stand. A murderer comes over and beats me without cease: – You dog, my whip is broken by this time every day, but today it's still in one piece!

He beats me without stopping. I am foaming at the mouth and feel that my strength is at an end. The same is true of my friends. In the distance stands a murderer observing our work. He calls over one after another of us, tells each one to undress and descend into the pit. The victims have to bend over and receive a bullet in the head. They then fall on top of the corpses that lie spread out beneath them.

After about fifteen minutes perhaps twenty of my comrades are missing. Our group is thinning out. I look around and see that there is almost no-one left. I am sure that my turn will come in a few minutes. I don't know where I get the extraordinary strength to throw myself into my work, to the point where the murderer standing next to me and beating me says: – You work well. I won't shoot you.

I am unsteady on my feet and can't go on . . . The comrade working next to me begs me to keep going. He is a little stronger than I am and tries to make things easier for me. He fills my barrow with sand so I can have a minute to rest.

It is about 4.00 in the afternoon. Of the thirty fellow-inmates who came here, I see that no more than six remaining. One after the other had to undress, go down into the pit and receive a bullet in his head. We did not hear so much as a groan. Down in the pit stand two workers who lay out the dead.

Suddenly a new murderer appears. He tells us to put down our barrows and leads us to a different job. He tells us to take hold of what look like ladder-shaped litters. The litters are bloody. Two of us grab a litter and are driven to a distant building. In it are scattered piles of stiff bodies to a height of one storey. These are the people who were gassed.

We have no time to think because the whips fly over our heads. I don't know what to do. I look on for a while, then see how Jews come running with empty litters, put them down quickly and run over to the pile of corpses. One of them takes a dead body by one hand, a second by the other hand. They pull it off the pile, drag it onto the litter and run off as quickly as possible.

I try to do the same, but it is hard for me; I am stunned by the picture before my eyes. I grab the hand of a corpse that has several other corpses lying on top of it. My comrade grabs the corpse's other hand and we try to pull it out. But we cannot. One of the murderers sees that we have been standing there for several minutes and runs over and beats us without stopping. The blood is pouring down our faces. But we pay no attention to that and try to pull out another corpse. We succeed. Seeing how things are done, we drag the corpse quickly onto the bloody litter and run in the direction where everyone is running. Along the way we are once again accompanied by the whips of the murderers who stand on both sides. Being new, we don't orientate ourselves right away and are beaten even more.

Along the way stand the "dentists" who inspect every corpse to see if it has any gold teeth. Not knowing about this, I don't stop, because I'm afraid of being beaten. A dentist sees that the corpse I am carrying has gold teeth. He stops me and won't let me go any further since he has to extract the teeth. He shouts to me to stand still and blocks my path. I shout to him: – Why won't you let me run? I'll get whipped on account of you. He reassures me that by standing next to him I won't be beaten. He tells me quietly that if he lets a corpse with false teeth pass him by he will get a bullet in his head. I see how his hands are trembling. After a few seconds he tells me: – Now go!

I break into a line of carriers who are running with corpses one after another. We come to a deep pit and I try to imitate what the carriers running ahead of me are doing. I try, like them, to dump the corpse by tilting the litter to one side. But the head gets stuck between the rungs of the litter and we can't do anything about it. We try to pull out the head, but we are unable to. Meanwhile we are delaying those who are waiting behind us. The worker, a Jew, who lays the bodies out straight like herrings shouts to me to put the litter on the ground quickly and pull the head of the corpse out from between the rungs. A murderer standing near the pit runs over and rains down blows on us with his whip until we finally succeed in pulling out the head of the corpse and then run off with the empty litter in the direction of the heap of dead bodies.

During the time I am delayed by pulling out the head of the dead man the chain of workers is broken, and as the first to arrive I receive supplemental beatings. By now every part of my body is in pain and I am at a loss what to do.

We arrive at the grim mound. I throw the litter down quickly, I run over and pull off a corpse from the top layer. Though I see a bandit coming, intending to beat us, I pay no attention and throw the corpse face down onto the litter. The bandit detains and beats me.

A carrier running past shouts to me to put the litter down and turn the corpse right side up and make sure that the head is resting on a board, because if it lies between the rungs it will be stuck when the body is dumped. I put down the litter, turn the victim over, and we run off.

Running back and forth several times I finally see what things look like in the deep pit: several laborers stand in the pit, all of them Jews, and lay out the dead bodies one next to the other. That is how the work proceeds. The pit becomes more and more full. There can be no question of resting for a while because we have to run one after the other, without a break. We run back and forth. The two hours that pass in this way, until evening, seem like a year.

The clock strikes 6.00 We run one after the other to the shed where the litters and shovels are stored. All must be put away correctly, otherwise we get the whip.

Finally we assemble for roll-call. After being counted, to the accompaniment of music, we are driven into a barracks surrounded by barbed wire.

8

My comrade Yankl chooses me for his partner to carry corpses.
A sweet dream about my dead mother. The avenue of hanged Jews.
The columns march out to work. My comrade's bloody drink.
The jump into the well.

I fall over and cannot move. I lie there for a while and hear a shout from the kitchen, ordering us to go and get our coffee. I can barely stand. We are driven from the barracks and once again line up in groups of five to proceed to the kitchen. It takes a couple of minutes before the little window is opened. One after the other we receive a piece of bread and a little muddy water which is called coffee. I have a burning thirst and drink all the coffee without eating the bread, despite the fact that I am starving. The eating ends and we go back to the barracks. I am like a dead man myself. I look around and see that each of us is bruised and bloody.

Groans are heard from all sides. Everyone weeps over his

wretched fate. I lie in pain and weep for what I have lived to see. Next to me lies another man who groans just as much as I do. I try to find out something about him. He tells me he is from Częstochowa and that his name is Yankl. We become friendly and he tells me a secret, which is that he has been here for ten days. He points out that no-one knows this because none of us know each other. It is very rare for a labourer to last as long as he has. Every day tens of labourers are shot and new labourers are taken from the most recent transports. That way none of us get to know each other. He tells me that two days ago more than a hundred labourers were shot. He informs me that whoever has a bruise on his face is doomed. For that reason he advises me to pay attention and avoid receiving blows to the face insofar as possible. I tell him how many blows I have received and he laughs: here that is nothing new and he is used to it. But at every word he groans: – Oy, everything hurts . . .

I ask him if we can carry a litter together. He doesn't want to, because he will get additional beatings as a result of my inexperience. I beg him and promise that I will adapt myself to his routine and do everything he tells me to do. He finally agrees and advises me that at roll-call the next morning I should stand next to him, because running to work is a veritable madhouse and whoever is left without a partner gets whipped.

We continue to talk for a while, and my friend Yankl falls asleep on the hard boards. I lie there and feel every part of me aching. I don't know how I will be able to get up in the morning. I lie there and think: Where am I actually? In Hell, a Hell with demons. We wait for death, which can come at any moment, in a few days at best. And for the price of a few days of life we have to dirty our hands and help the bandits do their work. No, we must not do it!

I fall asleep and dream of my honest, faithful mother, who died fifteen years ago. I was fifteen years old at the time. My mother weeps with me over our fate. She died young. She was thirty-eight when she was torn from us and left us behind. To await such a death? Would it not have been better if the rest of us had not survived? How good it is that my mother did not live to be tortured, to experience a ghetto, poverty, hunger and, at the end, Treblinka: to have her hair torn away, to be gassed, then tossed into a pit like tens of thousands of other dead people. I am happy that she did not live to see that.

My headache wakes me up. Everything hurts and I cannot lie still. I try to turn over and unintentionally bump into my friend Leybl. He wakes up and cries: – Murderer, what do you want from me? I try to apologize, but he answers with a groan: – Oy, oy . . . I try not to touch him again. I want to fall asleep, but I cannot. The night passes slowly like a year, until finally we hear the shout: – Aufstehen! (Get up!) People tear themselves out of their sleep, and everyone tries to stand near the door, which is still closed.

I notice that opposite me is dangling a man who has hanged himself. I point this out to my neighbour, but he waves dismissively and shows me that further along there are two more people hanging: – That is nothing new here. Actually today there are fewer hanging that usual. He tells me that every day several bodies of hanged men are thrown out and nobody pays attention to such details.

I look at the hanging bodies and envy them for being at rest. After a short while the door is thrown open and we are driven out to the kitchen. We get coffee and I still have the piece of bread from yesterday. Most of the Jews just drink the black coffee. The clock strikes 5.30 and we hear a shout: – Antreten! (Fall in!) We all run out. I see how each of us tries to stand next to someone to make a pair and I try to stand next to my comrade. Fortunately we are standing together.

As usual we are counted quickly. The gate is opened and we are let out: first, a group that works in the machine shop. Those are the mechanics who work on the automobile engine from which the gas is piped to the gas chambers. They rush off to work because a transport has arrived and the preparations to receive it must get under way.

Then the dentists' group is let out. They run immediately into their cell. They have to get their dental pliers quickly and run to the open space in order to inspect the bodies and extract the false teeth of the dead.

After the dentists the carpenters are let out. Their work consists of building barracks and interior structures.

After them comes the Schlauch (feeder tube) group. Their job consists of removing the blood of the victims spilled on the way to the gas chambers. Everything is covered with sand so no trace will remain. After cleaning the road they enter the gas chambers and wash the walls and floors. There must be no trace of blood. The entrances to the gas chambers are opened and a painter gives the walls a fresh coat of paint. Everything must be spotless before receiving new contingents in the cells.

After the *Schlauch* workers comes the *Rampe* (ramp) group. Those are the Jews who work at the gas chambers when a transport has already been gassed. At a signal, the exterior doors are opened and it is time for the *Rampe* workers to remove the corpses. This work is extraordinarily difficult, as the dead are tightly pressed against one another.

After the *Rampe* workers, the group of kitchen workers comes out. The remaining inmates are then counted. Some of them are assigned to carry corpses and the rest are sent to the sand piles. I notice that the workers who have been here for several days try to avoid the work of carrying sand, because the *Scharführer* (section chief) of the sand workers, nicknamed "The White Man", is a specialist in shooting. At roll-call he often shows up by himself because he has shot his workers down to the last man.

My friend and I work as carriers. The day, as usual, is extraordinarily difficult. We receive so many lashes that our feet can no longer carry us. A sip of water is not to be had. Our lips burn with thirst. It is no use begging or crying. All you get are blows, blows without end.

My comrade with whom I'm carrying a litter notices, while

standing for a moment near one of the dentists, that the bowl into which the dentist throws the bloody teeth contains a little water. He throws himself to the ground and drinks the water together with the blood. He gets whipped, but he drinks.

The day is especially difficult. There is a transport today of eighteen thousand people, and all the gas chambers are active.

We work. From time to time it happens that carriers throw down their litters and jump into the deep well that stands near the death chambers and in that way end their accursed lives.

Finally the clock strikes 6.00. There is a shout – Antreten! – and we fall in. Our Scharführer, Mathias, orders us to sing a pretty song. We have to sing. It is almost an hour before we return to the barracks.

9

I join the dentists' commando. Forty hours in the gas chambers.
The mad rush before and after the gassing of the victims.
The technique of dental work. I am whipped for letting
through a corpse with false teeth.

After four weeks of working as a carrier, I succeeded in getting into the dentists' commando. There were nineteen dentists and I was the twentieth.

When *Scharführer* Mathias returned from leave, he ascertained at roll-call that there were nineteen men in the group of dentists. He ordered the *Kapo* of the dentists, Dr Zimmermann, an acquaintance of mine, to raise the number to twenty. That was around 3 November [1942]. At that time the transports were increasing once again and more dentists were needed. When Dr Zimmermann announced that he was looking for a dentist, I stepped out and declared that I was a dentist. Other people also declared themselves as dentists, but Dr Zimmermann chose me and got me into his group.

We marched off to our work.

In the building containing the three smaller gas chambers there was an additional wooden shed, which was entered via the corridor that led to the gas chambers. In the shed stood a long table at which the dentists worked. In a corner of the shed stood a locked trunk in which were kept the gold and platinum crowns from the teeth of the corpses, as well as the diamonds that were sometimes found in the crowns, along with the money and jewels that were found under bandages on the naked bodies or in the women's vaginas. Once a week the trunk was emptied by Mathias or Karl Spetzinger, his adjutant. Next to the table stood long benches on which we used to sit tightly crowded together and do our work. On the table were placed dishes with extracted teeth as well as various dental tools.

Our work consisted of scraping out and cleaning the metal from the fillings and from the natural teeth. An additional task was to separate the crowns from the bridges and then clean and sort them. For that purpose there was a special blowtorch which melted rubber. The dentists were divided into specialized groups. Five men worked with white false teeth, others with metal teeth, and two specialists were occupied with sorting the metals, especially white gold, yellow gold, platinum and ordinary metal. The dentists used to sit at their work under the direction of Dr Zimmermann, who was a very decent human being. Germans used to come to him when they had some special business.

Before going on leave they used to come to us to pick out a couple of beautiful stones for themselves, or some foreign currency.

In the shed stood a small stove. In one wall there were two small windows which looked out onto the open space in front of the building with the ten big gas chambers. When a transport was brought in and the outer doors of the gas chambers were opened, the Germans would knock on the windows shouting: – *Dentisten raus!* (Dentists out!) Depending on the size of the transport, one or more groups of six men would go out to work. With pliers in their hands they would position themselves along the path via which the corpses were carried from the ramp to one or more of the mass graves. (When they began to incinerate the dead, they were carried to the ovens.)

It is worth mentioning that at the time I began working in the death camp, there were two gassing structures in operation. The larger one had ten chambers, into each of which as many as four hundred people could enter. Each chamber was 7 metres long by 7 metres wide. People were stuffed into them like herrings. When one chamber was full, the second was opened, and so on. Small transports were brought to the smaller structure, which had three gas chambers, each of which could hold 450 to 500 persons. In that structure the gassing would last about twenty minutes, while in the more recent structure it would last about three quarters of an hour.

On days when the gentlemen would learn by telephone from the extermination headquarters in Lublin that no new transports would be arriving the next day, the murderers, out of sadism, would let the people stand stuffed into the gas chambers so that they would be asphyxiated. On one occasion, when they had stood like that for forty-eight hours and the exterior doors were opened, a few people were still struggling and showing signs of life.

Most of the people became entirely swollen and black. The S.S. men or the Ukrainians would look in through the peep-holes to see if everyone was dead and if the rear doors could now be opened.

As I am standing at work at the table and beginning to get the hang of using the tools, we hear the above-mentioned knocking at our windows. Our group leader already has noticed that the ramp is starting to work, that the special ramp commando is about to open the doors. He appoints six men to go out onto the path along which the carriers run with the corpses. He has included me.

Each member of the group takes two pairs of pliers. We then go outside to the transport. From the carpentry workshop, where among the carpenters is Yankl Wiernik (a survivor whose *A Year in Treblinka* was published in New York in 1944 by Unser Tsait), each one of us grabs a bowl. In our shed there is no room for the bowls, so they are kept in the carpenters' room. A whole stack of them lies there. Each of us grabs a little water at the well and runs to work.

At the open space in front of the ramp the scene is an inferno.

The rear door has been opened. When it is opened, deadly fumes are emitted from inside. The corpses, all standing, are so tightly pressed together and have their hands and feet so intertwined that the ramp commando are in danger of their lives until they are able to pull out the first few dozen corpses. Then the mass of bodies loosens and the corpses start to fall out by themselves. The tight compression sometimes results from the fact that people are terrorized and crammed in as they are driven into the gas chambers, so that everyone has to hold his breath in order to be able to find a bit of space. During their death agonies from asphyxiation the bodies also become swollen, so the corpses form literally a single mass.

There was a difference in the appearance of the dead from the small and from the large gas chambers. In the small chambers death was easier and quicker. The faces often looked as if the people had fallen asleep, their eyes closed. Only the mouths of some of the gassed victims were distorted, with bloody foam visible on their lips. The bodies were covered in sweat. Before dying, people had urinated and defecated. The corpses in the larger gas chambers, where death took longer, were horribly deformed, their faces all black as if burned, the bodies swollen and blue, the teeth so tightly clenched that it was literally impossible to open them, and to get to the gold crowns we had sometimes to pull out the natural teeth – otherwise the mouth would not open.

The work of clearing out the corpses was divided up. In addition to the ramp men (about twenty in number), forty to fifty carriers were employed, six dentists and, at the pits, a commando of grave-diggers. About ten of the latter stood in the pit and worked at laying out the corpses head to foot and foot to head so that the maximum number went in. A second group covered the corpses with sand, whereupon a second layer was laid down.

The pits were dug by a bulldozer (later on there were three of them). The pits were enormous, about 50 metres long, about 30 wide and several storeys deep. I estimate that the pits could contain about four storeys.

The movement, the running and chasing, the beatings constituted an infernal vicious circle. Over every group of workers stood several Germans or Ukrainians with whips in their hands, ceaselessly beating the Jews on their heads, backs, stomachs, hands, not much caring where the blows landed. If they did pay attention to the blows, it was to land them in a spot where it would hurt the most or where it could injure the body the most. The ramp men, the carriers and indeed everyone had to do their work at a fiendishly rapid tempo. The ramp men had to make sure that there was always a ready pile of corpses so the carriers would not have to wait. The carriers had to grab a corpse on the run (picking out a lighter specimen from afar), throw it on the litter and gallop with it to the pit.

The litters were in the shape of a ladder with a strap to pull over the shoulders.

The dentists stood in a row on the way from the ramp to the pit. The first in line had the function of quickly inspecting the mouth of the corpse, and, if he noticed gold or false teeth, of passing the corpse to one of the dentists down the line whose hands were free. The carriers stood aside for a moment in order not to interfere with the operation. It was not permitted to lay a corpse on the ground. The carriers then held the corpse, and the dentist quickly seized the tooth or bridge with his pliers and extracted it as fast as possible. Careful attention had to be paid not to miss a tooth that ought to have been extracted. At the pit the Germans would look and inspect. Woe to the dentist who had left a gold tooth in the mouth of a corpse.

I once experienced a case in which a German noticed a gold tooth sparkling in the mouth of a corpse. Since I was the last one standing in the row of dentists, the blame fell on me. I had to jump into the pit at once, rolling head over heels several times. I had to extract the tooth quickly, and when I climbed out again the S.S. man ordered me to stretch out on the ground and administered twenty-five lashes. Another time, somewhat later, I missed a whole mouthful of teeth. Once again I was the last one in the row. All the other dentists were busy, the corpse was very heavy, and the carriers who were hauling it thought they could throw it into the pit without it being inspected. Standing at his post at that time was *Unterscharführer* Gustav. He noticed unextracted teeth in the mouth of the corpse and thereupon the same scene was repeated. This time I received perhaps seventy lashes. He beat me on my back with all his strength, always in the same spot. He nearly severed my spinal cord. When with great difficulty I got up, blood was pouring over my body and into my trousers. On my back there was a big crust of blood; the next day it became apparent that I had blood poisoning. I would undoubtedly have died had it not been for Dr Zimmermann, who operated on me. It was my good fortune that it was a Sunday, when we were free from work. Dr Zimmermann had all his instruments with him and performed the operation in the barracks, even with anaesthesia. He opened the wound and cleaned it out, and in this way saved my life.

10

The Jews of Ostrowice are driven into the gas chambers at night.
They resist. The astonishment of Chief Mathias . . . A new form of
entertainment. People strive to get into the gas chambers.

Until 15 December [1942] the transports arrived regularly, approx-
imately ten thousand people a day. If a transport arrived after 6.00
in the evening, its passengers were not gassed that day. The transport was kept at Treblinka station and only on the next day was it
brought into the camp.

As it happened, on 10 December a transport of Jews from
Ostrowice was waiting at the station. The camp administration
was advised that the next morning a new transport would be
brought to Treblinka. The *Kommandant* gave the order that the
Jews of Ostrowice should be brought in at night. The order was
carried out. By then we were locked in our barracks and could see
nothing. We only heard the usual screams. But when we went out

to work the next morning, we saw traces of the events of the previous night. The ramp men opened the rear doors and began to pull out the corpses. The carriers carried them to the pits. But this time the carriers and cleaning crew of the so-called *Schlauch* commando had an additional task.

The whole corridor of the structure with the three smaller gas chambers was filled with dead bodies. The floor was covered with ankle-deep dried blood. We learned from the Ukrainians what had happened there. A group of about ten men who were being driven into the chambers had refused to go. They resisted and, naked as they were, defended themselves with their fists and did not allow themselves to be shoved into the chambers. Whereupon the S.S. men opened fire with automatic weapons, killing them on the spot.

The ramp men carried out the corpses, the cleaning crew washed down the corridor, the painters as always whitewashed the walls that had been covered with the blood and brains of the dead, and the building once again stood ready to receive new victims.

Afterwards the section chief, Mathias, came over to us, the dentists, and called out to our group leader, Dr Zimmermann: – Did you know, Doctor, that those chaps tried to cheat us?

Mathias was truly astonished. He could not grasp why the Jews did not willingly let themselves be murdered. He found this an abnormal development.

That day was extraordinarily difficult. Soon after the first transport a second one arrived, and, as it happened, in that transport there were many gold and false teeth to extract.

After a certain number of corpses had been dealt with, the teeth were collected in two bowls, and two dentists would take them to the well and wash them before bringing them into our shed to be worked on. In our shed there was always a supply of teeth stored in chests, and if we had not cleaned them of blood and of the bits of flesh that stuck to them, they would begin to stink.

When there was a short pause in the work, when the cleaning crew had finished in one of the gas chambers but the second one was not yet done gassing and the victims inside still showed signs of life or one could still hear their screams, the beasts forced us to dance and sing songs to the accompaniment of the Jewish orchestra that stood next to our barracks and played without interruption.

In December the transports grew less frequent. Some of the Germans were on leave. Mathias had left even earlier and did not return till after New Year 1943. When he came back he looked much worse than he had before. It seems he felt better in Treblinka than he did at home. The air of Treblinka suited him. During the two days of Christmas there were no transports at all.

The transports began to arrive regularly once more around 10 January. That was a very difficult day. On that day fresh transports arrived. At the same time a "guest" came to us from Camp 1, *Obersturmführer* Franz, nicknamed "Lyalke" (Doll). Together with him came his dog, Barry, who was just as notorious as his master.

Once work had resumed, the Germans began to apply new methods.

Around 10 January, transports began arriving from the borderlands of eastern Poland, from Białystok, Grodno and the surrounding areas. It was a hard winter with freezing temperatures. Now the sadists thought up a new form of entertainment. At a temperature of -20 Celsius they would keep rows of naked young women outdoors, not allowing them to enter the gas chambers. The men and the older women having already been asphyxiated, the rows of young women, half frozen, stood barefoot in the snow and ice, trembling, weeping, clinging to one another and begging in vain to finally be allowed into the "warmth" where death awaited them.

The Ukrainians and Germans looked on with pleasure and mockery at the pain of the young bodies, joking and laughing, until at last they mercifully allowed them to enter the "baths". Such scenes were repeated in the following days and continued throughout the winter.

It is worth mentioning that in winter the extraction of teeth became much more difficult. Whether it was because the corpses froze when the doors were opened, or the result of the freezing of the victims on the way to the gas chambers, the opening of their clenched mouths was fiendishly difficult for us. The more we struggled, the more the murderers knocked us over and beat us.

In general, even in summer, the victims tried to arrive at the gas chambers as quickly as they could during the final passage along the *Schlauch*. The gas chambers offered protection from the beatings, and people wanted to get everything over with as quickly as possible.

In February 1943 great piles of ash began to accumulate as a result of the decision to begin burning the corpses. A special ash commando was organized. In the morning, when everyone went out to work, the carriers, working in stages, would put the ashes from the furnace grills into crates that were attached to the litters. (These crates were also used when corpses taken from the pits to be incinerated were in such a state of decomposition that they could not be placed on the ladder-shaped litters but had to be thrown piece by piece into the crates.) The carriers dumped the ashes in piles, and it was at these piles that the specially organized ash commando now worked. The work of the ash commando was as follows:

The body parts of the corpses that had been incinerated in the ovens often kept their shape. It was not uncommon to take out whole charred heads, feet, bones etc. The workers of the ash commando then had to break up these body parts with special wooden mallets which recalled the iron mallets used to pound gravel on motorways. Other instruments resembled the tools used when working with sand and stone. Near the heaps of ash stood thick, dense wire meshes, through which the ashes were sifted, just as sand is sifted from gravel. Whatever did not pass through was beaten once more. The beating took place on sheet metal which lay nearby. The carriers were not allowed to bring bones from the grills that had not been completely incinerated. They remained lying next to the furnaces and were thrown on top of the next layer of corpses that were brought in. The definitive "finished" ash had to be free of the least bit of bone and as fine as cigarette ash.

When great piles of this kind of finished ash had accumulated, the Germans began to carry out various experiments with a view to getting rid of it and erasing every trace of the murders that had taken place. They tried in the first instance to convert the ash into "earth" with the help of special liquids. Experts arrived and, standing over the ash heaps, mixed the ashes with sand in various proportions. Then they poured in some sorts of liquids out of bottles. But the results did not satisfy them. After the experiments they decided to bury the ash deep in the ground under thick layers of sand.

A shallow layer of ash was poured into the deep pits from which the corpses had been exhumed, then on top of that a shallow layer of sand, and so forth until they had reached the level of about 2 metres below the surface. The last 2 metres were filled only with sand. In this way they reckoned that they would erase forever the traces of their horrible crimes.

The Jewish workers who were employed in the emptying of the pits nevertheless used every opportunity to leave behind in the earth some remains of human bones. Since the pits became narrower as they grew deeper, and the earth along the sides would crumble, every time the Germans and their informers were absent the workers would bury as many bones as they could beneath a layer of sand.

The ash was poured in shallow layers – a layer of ash and a layer of sand. That was the usual procedure. The carriers who delivered the ash and sand from morning till night firmly tamped down the surface with their feet.

I remember that every morning when we went out to work, we would notice that the surfaces of the pits had burst in dozens of places. By day the ground was firmly trodden down, but at night the blood pressed up to the surface. This raised the level to such an extent that in the morning the carriers sweated with exertion while descending into the pits with their loads of ash and sand.

The blood of tens of thousands of victims, unable to rest, thrust itself upwards to the surface.

II

Obersturmführer *Franz and his dog, Barry. The murderers
drink to the arrival of the British Jews. A new "specialist".*

It is a beautiful day. The murderers are in a good mood. Our
section chief, Mathias, sits down on an embankment along with
his distinguished guest, deputy *Kommandant Obersturmführer* Franz,
whom we call "Lyalke" (Doll). This Lyalke is a terrible murderer.
His appearance at the open space in the camp triggers extraordinary fear. His specialty is slapping. From time to time he calls a
worker over, tells him to stand at attention and gives him a powerful slap on his cheek. The victim then has to fall down and immediately get up, in order to receive a slap on the other cheek. Then
he calls over his dog, Barry, who is almost as big as a man, and
shouts: – Man, bite that dog! The dog is very obedient to his friend
the deputy *Kommandant* and attacks the Jew.

Our section chief, Mathias, invites the criminal to sit down for a while and observe how well the work is proceeding. Lyalke sits down, and they converse, smiling.

They are in a good mood and pleased that the work is moving along at a brisk pace.

Their hearts swell with pride as they watch the living corpses running without interruption, like demons. Everyone is at his post, and in fact when they are not present the work goes even better than usual. Their collaborators flog with their whips ceaselessly, ceaselessly . . .

The murderers are content. Our section chief orders a Ukrainian to bring him a good bottle of cognac from the canteen. It doesn't take long before his wish is fulfilled. They fill the first goblet, and the guest, Lyalke, says: – We drink to the imminent arrival of the Jews of England!

The section chief is very pleased with the joke and laughs: – Ja, das ist gut, das kommt sicher! (Yes, that's good, that's sure to happen!)

In winter the criminals leave the women destined for the gas chambers outside at a temperature of -25 degrees Celsius. The snow is half a metre high and the murderers laugh: – How beautiful it is!

In December 1942 the criminals began to set up ovens to burn the corpses, but they did not work well, as the corpses refused to burn. For that reason a crematorium was built with special fittings. A special motor was attached that increased the flow of air, and in addition a lot of petrol was poured in. But the corpses still do not want to burn well. The maximum number of incinerated corpses reaches a thousand per day. The murderers are not satisfied with this small quantity.

We wondered, unable to understand, why the murderers had begun to look for ways to burn the corpses of the people they had gassed. After all, we had kept on digging deeper and deeper pits, but now the tactics had changed. By pure chance we found out the reason: one of the murderers gave us a present of a piece of bread wrapped in newspaper. That was an extraordinary event for us. From the articles in the newspaper we learned that the German authorities had discovered, in Katyń, near Smolensk, the graves of ten thousand Polish officers who supposedly had been murdered by the Soviets. We understood that the murderers wanted to blacken the name of Soviet Russia and were therefore starting to burn the corpses so no trace of what they had been doing would remain.

In January [1943] a new "specialist" came to our camp. We nicknamed him "Artist", since he plays his role so well. He is an extraordinary disposer of corpses. From the first moments of his arrival he is to be found at the pits. He laughs at the sight of them and is happy and satisfied with his role.

After a few days he gets to work intensively. He orders the ovens to be dismantled and laughs at how things are done here. He assures our section chief that from now on the work will go much better. He lays down ordinary long, thick iron rails to a length of 30 metres. Several low walls of poured cement are built to a height of 50 centimetres. The width of the oven is a metre and a half. Six rails are laid down, no more. He orders that the first layer of corpses should consist of women, especially fat women, placed with their bellies on the rails. After that anything that arrives can be laid on top: men, women, children. A second layer is placed on top of the first, the pile growing narrower as it rises, up to a height of 2 metres.

The corpses are thrown up by a special commando called the fire commando. Two fire-workers catch every corpse that is brought to them by the corpse carriers. One catches a hand and foot on one side, the second catches the other side, and then they throw the dead person into the oven. In this way some twenty-five hundred corpses are piled on. Then the specialist orders dry twigs placed underneath and lights them with a match. After a few minutes the fire flares up so strongly that it is difficult to get any closer to the oven than 50 metres. The first fire is lit, and the test is successful. The camp administration show up, and all of them shake the hand of the inventor. But he is not pleased with the fact that for the time being only one oven is working. Therefore he orders that the excavator that was used to dig the graves should now start digging out the corpses that have been lying in the ground for months . . .

The excavator starts to dig out the dead – hands, feet, heads. The Artist, being a specialist, orders the machine operators to dump the remains in circles, so that the carriers with their litters (these are now different litters, box-like in shape, so that nothing will fall out of them while running fast) can quickly run over, grab the human body parts with their hands, throw them into the litters and carry them quickly to the ovens.

The work is now even harder than before. The stench is terrible. The workers are sprayed with the fluid that trickles from the cadavers. Often the excavator driver deliberately heaves the body parts onto the workers and bloodies them. It sometimes happens that our section chief, seeing that a worker is lying bloodied on the ground, asks him why. When he answers that he was injured by the excavator while dumping the cadavers, he receives several lashes as well.

But the Artist walks around half-mad with rage because work still is not proceeding as well as he would like it to.

Soon afterwards, two new excavators are brought into the camp. The joy of the murderers knows no limits, since now the work will proceed *tadellos* (flawlessly). The next day all the excavators begin to function. For us this is simply hell, since the same number of workers now have to serve three corpse processors. Each time, the machines throw out dozens of corpses and we have to carry them immediately to the oven.

The criminal specialist also introduces a modification of the work. He creates a special commando of several workers whose job consists of tossing the dead onto the carriers' litters. He does this so that the carriers will not have to deposit the litters on the ground and in the process waste several minutes. The throwers fill the litters, tossing the body parts of the dead with pitchforks so that the carriers, who pick up their litters in the morning, will have no possibility to rest for a moment until evening.

It turns out that the corpses dug out of the pits burn even better than those of recently gassed people. Every day new ovens are constructed, more and more of them. After a few days there are six of them. Each oven is served by several workers who load it with material.

The Artist is still not satisfied. He sees that the work is hampered by the intense fire, which does not let anyone get close to the oven. The work plan is therefore changed. The ovens are loaded by day and are lit at 5.30 in the evening.

12

About 250,000 corpses are burned. Transports of Jews from Bulgaria.
The music plays . . .

It is March 1943. The work proceeds ever faster. The section chief
orders that the excavators should be ready two hours before roll-
call, so that we won't have to wait. One grave after another is
cleared. If a pit has been cleared but a pool of blood has collected
in a corner, a worker had to strip naked, descend into the pit, and
scour the pit with his hands, looking for body parts.

From day to day the work improves. The ovens are moved from
place to place, closer to the pits, so that the path is shorter and less
time is wasted. It once happened that an oven was moved close to
a huge grave where perhaps a quarter of a million people were
buried. As usual the oven was loaded with the proper number of
bodies and in the evening it was lit. But a strong wind carried the
fire over to the huge grave and engulfed it in flames. The blood of

some quarter of a million people began to flare, and thus burned for a night and a day. The whole camp administration came to look upon this marvel, gazing with satisfaction at the blaze. The blood came up to the surface and burned as if it were fuel.

I remember 29 March. This day has remained etched in my memory: our comrade Yankl from Częstochowa lay down to sleep and did not wake up in the morning. Each of us wished for such good fortune. We accompanied him to the flames, threw him onto the burning corpses and cremated him.

It has been raining since morning without interruption. But we have to work. Each of us is soaked. The murderers take cover under the eaves and shout to us from there: – Faster, keep up the pace! From time to time an S.S. man runs over and whips us. Although the soil is sandy it turns muddy, and it becomes hard for us to run. The section chief orders us to bring several dozen litters of ash from the ovens and spread it on the ground. The mud absorbs the human blood. From time to time we have to add ashes, because it keeps raining harder. The day weeps along with us.

Since three excavators are in operation, the carriers are divided into three groups. It sometimes happens that one excavator breaks down and it takes several minutes to fix it. We likewise come to a halt. The Artist appears and good-naturedly inquires why we are standing around doing nothing while at the ovens there is a great deal of ash that needs to be carried away. Our group foreman points out that the excavator will soon be repaired. The

Artist answers that we will have time to carry away at least one voluntary round of ashes (he calls it an "*Ehren-Runde*").

The month of April began with fresh transports from abroad, especially Bulgaria.

In the early hours the section chief appears, orders the gas chambers to be shut and tells us that if we work well we will be fed well. Not long afterward we again hear cries of "Help, help" and "*Shema Yisroel*". After a few minutes the screaming from the gas chambers is silenced, and after half an hour – newly gassed people.

I look at the gassed people: they look very different from us. It's as if they had been specially selected for their youth and beauty. I have seldom seen among our Jews such healthy, beautiful bodies. Even after being gassed they look as if they are still alive, just asleep.

They were brought here in special Pullman cars. They even brought furniture with them, and a lot of food. Until the last minute they believed that they were being resettled in Russia for work. Their valuables were taken away from them and put in the so-called "deposit". The people, seeing that all the valuables were being thrown onto a single pile, pointed out that mistakes would be made when retrieving the objects after the baths, since no notes were being made of what belonged to whom. Yes, the murderers already knew to whom the things would belong – to the *Herrenvolk* (master race).

We learned from some workers from Camp 1 that when the

transport of Bulgarian Jews arrived, music was playing. The Jews were convinced that nothing bad would happen to them. As they exited the train, they asked if this was the big industrial complex known as Treblinka . . .

The S.S. man Karl Spetzinger appears and warns us dentists that we be particularly attentive, because almost every one of the Bulgarians has false teeth.

We find it difficult to cope, since in fact each one of them has a mouth full of false teeth. We have to pull hard, and the carriers weep because the corpses are exceptionally heavy. The murderers are beside themselves because the dentists are detaining almost every corpse. They start beating us. The section chief declares that if the "shit" is not removed by 4.00 in the afternoon, we will get no food. That day we work without food as a punishment.

A few minutes after 4.00 there remains no trace of the young and beautiful Bulgarian Jews.

13

An even bigger oven is built. Several days without transports. News
of the revolt in the Warsaw Ghetto. The traces of murder are effaced.
The earth is planted with lupins. Himmler's visit to Treblinka.

In the second half of April the staff appears with our section chief,
Mathias, at its head. We see that they have brought plans with
them, and at the same time they measure a section of terrain a few
metres from the ten big gas chambers. The next morning several
workers are chosen, and under the command of an S.S. man they
begin to dig several metres from the gas chambers. It turns out
that they are starting to build a much bigger and stronger oven
right next to the gas chambers, in order to be able to burn the
corpses at once. This work goes on for ten days. Apparently they
are expecting many transports. By now we have arrived at the last
days of April and the oven is still not ready. The section chief
orders that a new oven be erected close to the gas chambers in a

few days. The gas chambers are sealed in preparation. But the day is a happy one for us, because no transports arrive. We notice how the murderers run around like mad dogs; they beat, they scream like scalded pigs.

In the evening we heard the whistle of a locomotive. But it turned out that it was a freight train. Another day went by and no transports arrived. The murderers are furious. We are unable to find out what has happened. Three days pass in this way. On the third day the section chief orders the gas chambers reopened. For the first time in Treblinka it happened that the gas chambers were sealed in readiness but no transports came.

In a few days the chambers were sealed again and a few days later a transport came. Almost all of the murderers were present to receive the arrivals. Each of them had a whip in his hand, and Ivan was holding his 3-metre bar.

I am in the dentists' shed. I hear the pitiful screams. The murderers are wild. They have selected three women from the transport to work in the laundry. We believe that they deliberately sent the women to us so that we would know what happened to the Jews of Warsaw.

The three women were in a daze for three days and did not understand what we said to them. After a few days they calmed down a bit and told us that the Jews of Warsaw resisted heroically and did not let themselves be killed off, that the Ghetto was in flames and that the Jews were fighting with weapons in their hands.

It saddens us to hear from the women that the Ghetto was in flames. But the women are proud when they tell how the Jews fought and that there were German casualties as well.

We are heartbroken by the news, but at the same time the will and determination rise up in us to free ourselves from Treblinka.

The work proceeds at a rapid pace. It seems as if they have a deadline by which everything here should be liquidated. No sooner is one pit emptied than the next one is dug.

The Artist, seeing that there are still whole corpses in the upper layers of the mass graves, gives orders to drop the litters, pick up the corpses by hand and burn them in the ovens. Each carrier tries to utilize the moment when the machine descends into the pit to run over, grab a corpse and run away again, thereby avoiding being hit by the falling corpses that the excavator throws up.

The corpses are counted by special workers. Every evening they have to report to Section Chief Mathias how many corpses were burned. Only whole corpses are counted – those which still have the head attached. If the head is missing, the corpse does not count. Heads are counted separately. The section chief is under the impression that he is being cheated, that the counting is not being carried out correctly. He beats the workers and threatens to have them shot.

We dentists have a lot of work. There are several big chests filled with teeth. We have to clean them and every couple of days deliver a suitcase of dental gold, other gold and precious stones.

From time to time we receive visits from the *Kommandant* of

Treblinka. He speaks calmly and requests of our foreman that if we find a big, beautiful stone, we should give it directly to him. (Normally Section Chief Mathias takes such things to the camp coffers. The gold and valuables are sent, we have heard, directly to the *Reichsbank* in Berlin, where the dental gold is smelted into ingots.) The *Kommandant*, however, wishes to have such a stone for his own house museum as a souvenir . . . His request is easily fulfilled, since we are used to giving such stones to his assistants, hoping thereby to avoid extra beatings.

From time to time it happens that one of the murderers brings us a loaf of bread or a few cigarettes, which are then divided into twenty parts.

In May a new S.S. man arrives, and on the following day he comes into the dentists' shed to have his wristwatch repaired. A worker among us is a watchmaker by trade and fixes his watch. Our foreman takes advantage of the opportunity to ask for several suitcases from Camp 1. The S.S. man promises, not knowing that no-one from Camp 1 is allowed to come here. In the afternoon the German returns in the company of a worker from Camp 1, bringing several suitcases. He wants to send the worker back, but at the gate he is detained by Section Chief Mathias, who glares at the S.S. man and berates him for not knowing that no-one from Camp 1 is allowed to come here. He tells the worker to turn around, undress and go down into the pit, where he shoots him.

In June fewer transports arrive. The new oven is ready. Corpses are speedily thrown into it. The work of clearing out the pits likewise proceeds at a rapid pace. Ten pits have already been entirely cleaned out. The last, the eleventh, pit is one of the four biggest, where a total of a quarter of a million people lie. Two excavators work at this pit. A special commando is created, called the "*Knochen-Kolonne*" (Bone Brigade). Their task is to walk around with a bucket and pick up the tiniest bones, so that no trace will remain. The supervisor points out that if the greatest care is not taken, it will be considered sabotage. What that means does not have to be explained to any of us.

The third excavator, which is not in use for digging up corpses, begins to move earth from one place to another. Several workers assigned to the excavator have to keep an eye out for bones or other body parts and immediately bring them to the oven. The earth is turned over twice, so that no trace should remain.

By the end of June the space of the eleven pits, where hundreds of thousands of bodies had lain, was completely cleared. The earth was smoothed out and sown with lupins.

As became clear, the murderers had a deadline: 1 July for Camp 1. We learned that on that day we were expecting a notable guest – Himmler. Great preparations were made to receive him. The work was completed two days ahead of schedule.

It is the first of July. We were supposed to work in the afternoon. At the last minute, however, work was called off.

We lie confined to our barracks and see through the little windows that a strong guard has been placed around the building. A few minutes later Himmler arrives with his entourage. They inspect the gas chambers and head for the open space, which by then has been made neat and clean. Himmler apparently is satisfied. He smiles, and his accomplices beam with joy.

Several shots are heard – a signal of victory.

It is worth mentioning that among the S.S. men in Treblinka there were some who had come from the working class, former members of the Communist Party. One S.S. man was a former Evangelical pastor.

14

It was a hot day . . . "Trinkets". Mikolai and Ivan.
The murderer Zacke-Zacke.

It was a hot day. Several staff members had returned to the camp who had gone on leave a fortnight earlier, though every one of these bandits receives twenty-four days of leave every six weeks because of their strenuous "work". While on leave, they had dressed in civilian clothes and left their sacred uniforms in the camp. When they came back from their *Erholung* (recuperation) they were constantly in a bad mood. We once overheard a conversation in which one of them told the other that the city he comes from was being bombed day and night and that there were many casualties from air raids. We also notice that the murderers, coming back from leave, don't look good. It appears that the care they get at home is not as good as what they get in Treblinka. Here, in Treblinka, they can afford everything, since there is no lack of money. After all, every victim that arrives in Treblinka has managed to bring something with them.

It is a very difficult day today. S.S. *Unterscharführer* Chanke – we call him "The Whip" because he is a specialist in beating – is in a bad mood. His comrade *Unterscharführer* Loeffler is no small sadist himself. He has terrifying eyes, and all of us are afraid that his glance will fall on us because in that case we are done for. Despite the fact that they are tired from their journey, they beat us mercilessly.

I remember a case in which two workers forgot themselves and placed the corpses of three small children on the litter instead of one adult corpse. *Unterscharführer* Loeffler detained them, raining blows down on them from his whip and screamed: – You dogs, why are you carrying trinkets? ("Trinkets" is what they called little children.)

The "trinket"-bearers had to run back and collect an adult corpse.

On such a hot day the Ukrainian henchmen feel very good. They work left and right with their whips. Mikolai and Ivan, who work as mechanics on the motor that sends the gas into the chambers and also work on the generator that provides electric lighting for Treblinka, feel happy and in splendid shape in such weather. Ivan is about twenty years old and looks like a giant healthy horse. He is pleased when he has an opportunity to let off his energy on the workers. From time to time he feels the urge to take a sharp knife, detain a worker who is running past and cut off his ear. The blood spurts, the worker screams, but he must keep running with his litter. Ivan waits calmly until the worker runs back and orders him to put the litter down. He then tells him to strip and go over to the pit, where he shoots him.

Ivan once came over to the well where I and another dentist called Finkelstein were washing teeth. Ivan was carrying an auger. He ordered Finkelstein to lie down on the ground and drilled the iron tool into his buttocks. That was meant to be a joke. The wretched victim did not even scream, only groaned. Ivan laughed and shouted repeatedly: – Lie still, otherwise I'll shoot you!

Among the faithful Ukrainian helpers there are several heroes of this type. Etched in my memory is the Ukrainian we called "Zacke-Zacke" because when beating people he always yelled: – Zacke, zacke! (roughly: Pow, pow!) He has a special whip that is longer than all the other whips. Zacke-Zacke is on duty today. He has special privileges. He chooses the gate as his post. Here the entrance is narrow and it is convenient for him to beat people because he has everyone in his sight and it is impossible to avoid him. Zacke-Zacke is wild. Sweat pours down his diabolical face. The workers cry and he beats. In such cases Dr Zimmermann, who knew Russian, would try to distract him. Sometimes that was the only remedy that would cause him to leave off beating people for a while.

After the episode with Loeffler, Finkelstein had to get up and go back to work. He was a healthy young man. At the first opportunity Dr Zimmermann took him into his room and washed and bandaged his wound. The wound healed; Finkelstein survived till the revolt.

15

Life in the barracks. The typhus epidemic. The Lazarett.

Our life is difficult and filthy. We work from 6.00 in the morning until 6.00 in the evening. After work we are so tired that we fall to the ground exhausted. Not even a drop of water is to be had in the barracks, because the well is far away in the open space and after work we are driven into the dirty barracks, which are surrounded by barbed wire. Around it stands a special watch to guard us . . .

Treblinka is guarded by 144 Ukrainians and about a hundred S.S. men. They keep an eye on us like precious jewels. We are counted three times a day. But although every one of us is bruised and battered and every part of our bodies ache, not one of us dares to report himself sick. It often happens that the newly arrived workers don't know that you must not be sick and must never report during roll-call that you are ill. They are ordered to step out of line and undress on the spot. The murderers force them to do punishment exercises while naked, and then they are shot.

In Treblinka you must not be sick. Many of us cannot endure it and commit suicide. That is an ordinary event here. Every morning we notice that there are people hanging in the barracks.

I recall a father and son who had been in this hell for two days. They decided to commit suicide. Having only one strap between them, they agreed that the father would hang himself first and after that the son would take him down and use the same strap to hang himself. That is in fact how it happened. In the morning both were dead and we carried them out so that the chief murderer could verify that the number was correct.

It sometimes happens that as many as seventy workers are brought to us from a new transport. They work for a few hours until roll-call. The next day, at roll-call, they report that they are sick. The section chief assigns them to carry corpses. He hurries them along and makes them carry three corpses instead of one. They have to run fast, in step, and at the same time are brutally beaten on their heads. They are so exhausted that they cannot remain upright. After half an hour they are told to undress and are beaten some more. The murderers scream: – You dogs, you don't want to work! Then they order them to go over to the pit into which the corpses of the gassing victims are thrown. Each of the murderers wants to have the privilege of shooting. They agree among themselves that each of them should shoot several people.

They are pleased with this amusement and aim at the head. Seldom do two bullets have to be used for one victim.

In the early days, few of us knew each other, since every day new people arrived to take the place of those who had been shot. Later the murderers changed their tactics. Shooting workers soon after their arrival meant that the work went badly, since no-one had time to become accustomed to it.

We live here in filth. We wear our blood-covered shoes and clothes by day and by night we put them under our heads. We sleep crowded together, each one pressed against his neighbour. We have been wearing the same shirts we came here with and are covered with vermin. It is impossible to wash a shirt. The criminals shipped hundreds of waggons of clothing out of here, and we have nothing to wear. We suffer greatly from hunger. We receive only a small part of the food that the Jews brought with them. It reaches the point that the workers, finding a piece of bread in the chambers after the people have been gassed, do not hesitate to eat it.

In the middle of the twelfth month the work becomes more irregular. Fewer transports arrive and the work goes more slowly. Many of the S.S. men are on leave. At the same time a typhus epidemic breaks out in the camp, and many of the workers go around with a fever of 40 degrees Celsius. They can hardly stand, but are afraid to report that they are sick.

At a roll-call, the deputy chief of the camp, Karl Spetzinger (an S.S. man with the rank of *Scharführer*), announces that anyone who is sick can report to the doctor and nothing bad will happen to him. He will be able to remain in the barracks. At the same time he announces that the barracks located in the back row of the camp will be set up as a *Lazarett* (sick bay).

This arouses great fear, but nevertheless many people begin to report themselves sick because they can no longer stand. Over the course of several days the sick bay fills up. The number of sick people reaches about a hundred. I am among them. We lie there burning with fever. We receive no medical treatment. But it is good that we can lie there for a few days. The murderer has kept his word, just like all the criminal promises of the Germans.

After a few days, at 5.00 in the afternoon, several S.S. men give the order to expel ninety sick people from the *Lazarett*. The Ukrainians rush into the barracks and drag one person after another from their bunks by their feet. In about fifteen minutes the murderers have dragged out some eighty-odd sick people. They are not allowed to get dressed but take with them the blankets under which they have been lying. Of about a hundred sick people, thirteen are left. The rest are driven to the open space. A few minutes later, gunshots are heard . . .

We, the remaining few, are convinced that the next day it will be our turn to be shot. We therefore report that we are now healthy, and the doctor orders that we be given underwear. Each of us has to strip and wash himself. The door and windows of the barracks are open, the temperature is 20 degrees below freezing, and we wash ourselves. I want to get dressed, but I cannot stand upright. The same is true of my comrades. It is 4.00 in the afternoon and at 6.00 we have to go for roll-call. We are kept standing for an hour at roll-call, during which time we have to sing. The greatest music-lover of them all is the murderer Karl Spetzinger. He also likes recitations. Our comrade Spiegel, a former actor from Warsaw, has to recite to the accompaniment of the camp orchestra.

After this amusement we are told: – *Antreten! Rechts um!* (Fall in! Right turn!) We now also have to march in the open space. S.S. man Gustav, seeing that several comrades are barely able to walk, orders them to step out and shoots them. One of those called out, knowing what awaits him, steps out with a smile and bids us farewell in a loud voice: – I hope that you all will live to see what I have not lived to see.

The murderer flies into a rage and shoots him at once.

I try my best to lift my feet high. With a song we march half-dead into the barracks.

As a result of the filth, scabies began to appear. Almost all of us became sick with it. Having no medicines, we used ordinary brine. From that we get boils all over our bodies. The pain is unbearable. But in Treblinka you had to bear and survive that too . . .

16

We prepare for the revolt. Passover in the barracks.
The revolt in Treblinka.

As has already been mentioned, in the most recent period workers have been remaining where they were for longer than before.
This has been a great stroke of luck for us. As a result, we have
been able to get to know each other better. We have begun to trust
one another more and to think about the possibilities of escape.
We know that this is a difficult undertaking and are even afraid to
discuss it among ourselves for fear of denunciation. We examine
various possibilities. But the plans are difficult to carry out. We
are unarmed and yet we plan all sorts of things. Our conversations take place in the corners of the barracks, and there is always
a guard consisting of our own people to keep an eye out in case
one of the murderers comes into the barracks.

In January 1943, fifteen workers from Camp 1 are brought to

us. It often happens that instead of shooting people in Camp 1 they are brought to us to work with the corpses, which amounts to the same thing . . . a swift and certain death. Among the fifteen new workers, there are two, Adolf, a former sailor, and Zelo Bloch, a Czech Jew and an officer in the Czech army, who are devoted comrades. In a few days we become friends with them. They inform us that in Camp 1 they are planning a revolt. In that camp there are more possibilities, since a weapons store is located there. They therefore plan to make a copy of the key to the store-room and steal weapons. These two comrades are very energetic, devoted and honest. They console us and begin to work inten-sively. We make every effort to establish contact with Camp 1. It is very difficult, but we make the most of the opportunity created by the fact that several of us work at the *Schlauch* removing the blood of the murder victims. The *Schlauch* extends to the border of Camp 1, and there our people come in contact with the *Schlauch* workers from the other side. We succeed in reaching an understanding with them despite the fact that we are guarded by an S.S. man and a Ukrainian. Our method of communication is the following: a comrade speaks with another from our camp in a loud voice. The people from Camp 1 who are working nearby hear the conver-sation and respond in the same way – with a loud conversation among themselves. The criminals are particularly watchful to see that we do not speak to each other. I remember one case: after great effort we succeeded in persuading the section chief to allow several of our comrades who had brothers in Camp 1 to meet with them. His permission came with a warning: they may ask each other how they are. There can be no talking about work or about what our work consists of. The meeting took place in Camp 1. The conversations lasted at most for five minutes.

Our comrades came back content. Despite the fact that an S.S. man stood between each man and his brother, and that they were only permitted to speak German, they were nevertheless able to bring back some important news. The news was the following: in Camp 1 they had made a copy of the key to the weapons store and soon they would begin the work of liberation.

Our joy was indescribable. We, the broken cripples, gained new strength, and each of us wanted to believe that we would succeed.

In the meantime the work continues. Fifteen Jewish women are brought to us from a transport from Białystok. Some of them are to work in the kitchen, the rest in the laundry, which has been specially built. The sanitary conditions are being improved to a certain extent, and orders have been issued to give us a clean shirt every week, and warm water to wash with every Sunday. Life becomes a bit easier. At the same time a toilet is constructed, and a worker named Schwer, an engineer by profession, is assigned to it.

He is ordered to dress like a clown. He must wear a skullcap, a long black coat like a rabbi and a red scarf, and carry a black stick. In addition he has an alarm clock hung around his neck. This toilet supervisor is given the order that no-one can spend longer than two minutes in his toilet. If anyone sits there longer, he will be whipped. The camp chief often hides in a corner to observe how long people sit in the toilet and if the toilet supervisor is admitting only those who have numbers. We had to have special numbers to go to the toilet, and it often happened that the bandits refused to issue the numbers. You could be close to bursting, but instead of a number you got the whip.

The murderers like to amuse themselves at the expense of the toilet supervisor. He is constantly being given new things to wear so that he will look even funnier. He must clean the toilet wearing a rabbi's clothes. In the evening at roll-call he has to stand in his "uniform" and the murderers often ask him: – Rabbi, how goes it with the shit?

He must answer: – Very good!

The season of Passover is approaching. The murderers wish to turn it into a farce and give us flour for baking matzo and in addition a bottle of wine. A seder is prepared and the S.S. men come to our barracks as guests. Among us there is a cantor from Warsaw who bakes the matzos and directs the seder. The murderers poke fun at this comedy and after a few minutes they leave the barracks.

I recall the night of the seder: several comrades performed the ceremony. It was breezy outside, the ovens were burning, and the flames were flaring. That evening ten thousand Jews were burning; in the morning no trace would be left of them. And we carried out the seder according to all the rules.

The next morning, as we were starting work, the oven special-ist turned to us (as if anyone had asked him) and said that he knew very well that our work was very difficult and very dirty as well. So he pretended to ask us if we would like him to increase our number by fifty workers, thereby making our work easier. But he set the condition that we would receive the same food rations as before, which we would have to share with the new arrivals. He did not wait for our reply and said that he thought we would prefer to work a bit harder so long as our rations were not reduced. At the same time he assured us that it wouldn't be long before we were finished with this *Scheisse* and then life would be easier for us. Each of us would then receive a new set of clothes, and the work would become less arduous.

The next day we found out that what we were meant to have said was that the fine, clean life we would have after removing the traces of their criminal activity would be our deaths. The bandit came to us yet again and explained yet again that nothing bad would happen to us. We listened yet again and thought of our freedom . . .

We decide together with the workers in Camp 1 to blow up the camp. Not everyone knows. The decision is kept secret. Only the leaders and those comrades who have been assigned special tasks know.

The plan of the revolt is as follows: everyone will work norm-ally, very carefully, not revealing the least change in our routine. Everyone knows what his responsibility is. In order to carry out the plan, each of us must place himself close to his appointed task. When we hear two shots coming from Camp 1, that will be the signal for the revolt to begin. All of us are ready. Several comrades are assigned to set the gas chambers on fire. Others have the task of killing S.S. men and Ukrainians and seizing their weapons. Several men who work near the observation posts are to try and distract the Ukrainians there with pieces of gold.

All are at their assigned positions.

We, the dentists, have the task of gathering as much gold as possible to take along with us. We plan, upon escaping from our camp, to head in the direction of the Treblinka Labour Camp, which lies 2 kilometres away, in order to liberate the Jews and Christians interned there . . .

The plans are all in place, but unfortunately there is an unforeseen change: on the day chosen for the uprising, a transport arrives at 5.00 in the morning, and with it many S.S. men and Ukrainians. This ruins our plans and we are forced to postpone our action. We cannot get over this disaster. The fear in Camp 1 is very great, because they now have to return to the storehouse the weapons that were stolen with such difficulty. But they succeed in doing so and happily none of the murderers notice.

Difficult days begin for us. It is impossible to get anything done because we are surrounded by a strengthened watch.

In May the weather turns hot and the corpses being torn out of the ground cause the air to stink. The murderers cannot bring themselves to approach the pits. The excavator operators and S.S.

men choke on the foetid air. They are forced to change the work schedule, and instead of working from 6.00 in the morning we now must begin at 4.00 in the morning. The roll-call is at 3.30. We work until 2.00 in the afternoon without interruption. Then we receive the midday meal. It often happens that we have to keep working during the afternoon because new transports arrive.

We are constantly being hurried at work. The pits are emptied more and more every day. We let the people in Camp 1 know that if they do not advance the date for the uprising, we will have to do it ourselves before it is too late. We are divided in our opinions. One group is in favour of blowing up the camp ourselves. The other group is certain that if we act alone we are doomed to failure.

We cannot wait any longer. Every day seems like a year. We decide to give Camp 1 the latest date we can accept, and if we do not get a clear answer from them, we will under no circumstances wait any longer.

We receive from them only the answer that we should be patient and wait a few more days. Finally we receive a concrete reply from Camp 1: the uprising is set for 2 August, 4.30 in the afternoon. We wait impatiently for that day.

The morning of 2 August is beautiful. The sun is shining. All of us are feeling brave. Despite our fears, we are all happy that the time has come. There is a smile on everyone's face. We feel new strength, we feel more alive than ever. We go off to work with joy in our hearts, though we tell each other to try not to show it in our faces.

We prepare cans of benzene, supposedly for the motors. Our barracks leader, who works in the camp as a butcher, asks the camp deputy, Karl Spetzinger, for permission to sharpen his knives because we are to receive a dead horse and the knives are dull. Spetzinger agrees, and Kalman the butcher sharpens his knives and the pliers to cut the barbed wire.

Everything is ready. Our excitement is running high, but so is our fear that the murderers might find out something and shoot us. We fall out for the midday meal. The latest news from Camp 1 is that everything is ready. Our only concern is that something might happen once again to spoil our plans. We have seen to it that at every point, such as the ovens, there will still be people at work so that we will not be shut up in the barracks. We claim that the fires need attention, that they are not burning well. In the kitchen we supposedly haven't drawn enough water so we have to send several people back to get more. These are in fact three good soldiers. Their task, the moment the revolt begins, will be to cut the throats of the Ukrainian guards and seize their weapons.

The midday rations are being distributed. We are all hungry, as always, but none of us is able to eat anything. No-one asks for seconds of soup. Dozens of comrades do not touch the food. Afterwards all of us go back to work filled with happiness. We say to one another: – Ha-yom, ha-yom!" (Hebrew: The Day, the Day!)

The work goes quickly. The murderers are pleased that the work is humming along. We avoid speaking to one another so that no-one will notice anything. Our tools are hidden in the appropriate places.

Our comrade Adolf, using various pretexts, tries to check every position. Despite all our preparations, there are still many among us who have no idea what is supposed to happen. The time passes with extraordinary slowness. The fear that something may go wrong is unbearable.

The clock strikes 3.30.

We hear two gunshots from the direction of Camp 1 – a sign that the revolt has started. A few minutes later we receive the order to quit working. Everyone hurries to his post. A few seconds after that, flames engulf the gas chambers. They have been set on fire. The Ukrainian standing guard next to the barracks lies on the ground like a stuck pig, blood flowing from him. His weapon is already being used by our comrade Zelo. Shots are heard from all sides. The Ukrainians, whom our comrades have lured from the watchtowers, lie dead. Two S.S. excavator operators are dead. We head for the barbed wire shouting: – *Revolyutsya v Berline!* (Russian: Revolution in Berlin!) Several of the Ukrainians become disorientated and put up their hands. Their weapons are taken from them. We cut the wires one after the other. We are already at the third barbed-wire fence.

I am near the barracks. Many comrades have become confused and out of fear are hiding inside. I and several others urge them out, shouting: – Comrades, come out to freedom, faster, faster!

All are now outside. The third fence has been cut. Fifty metres further on there are trestles thickly interwoven with barbed wire. We try to cut these as well.

The firing of the murderers' machine guns can be heard now. Some of them have succeeded in getting hold of their weapons. At the trestles lie many of our comrades who became entangled in the wires and were unable to escape.

I am among the last to go. I am already outside. Next to me is Comrade Kruk, from Płock. He falls into my arms: – Comrade, we are free. We kiss one another. I manage to run a few dozen metres when I see that the murderers are coming after us with machine guns. An automobile is bearing down on us. On the roof is a machine gun shooting in all directions. Many fall down dead. There are dead bodies at every step. I change direction and run to the left off the road. The car continues along that Polish road and soon it is ahead of me. We run in various directions. The murderers pursue us from all sides.

I notice that the peasants working the fields and the shepherds are running away out of fear. Finally, having run about 3 kilometres, we find ourselves in a small woodland. We decide that there is no point in running further and hide in the dense brush. We number some twenty people. The group is too big, and we divide into two groups of ten men each. The groups are separated by about 150 metres.

We lie there for several minutes and suddenly see that Ukrainians with several S.S. men have surrounded the wood and are entering it. They encounter the second group and all of them are immediately shot.

Among us is a Czech called Masaryk, a nephew of the former Czech president Masaryk. His wife was Jewish and he accompanied her to Treblinka. When he sees that the murderers are closing in on us, he takes a razor blade from his pocket and slits his wrists. Blood spurts from his wrists. I try to stop him, but he cannot be dissuaded, out of fear of falling yet again into the hands of the murderers.

We lie quietly for a brief time. Fortunately, they have not noticed us and have left the wood. I bind Masaryk's wrists with a bit of linen and succeed in stanching the flow of blood. We lie there for a time, then notice that civilians have entered the wood. They apparently have noticed us and have turned back towards us. We decide to run away quickly. We run for several hundred metres and come to another wood. Evening falls and it grows dark. At midnight we proceed further, not knowing where we are going.

Masaryk, a former officer, is able to orientate himself at night by the stars. With him leading the way, we move on. We walk all night. At sunrise we find ourselves in a big, dense forest. We decide to stay there. We are exhausted and very hungry.

We lie there a whole day. We take turns every few hours to make sure that no-one snores loudly if he falls asleep since every rustle resounds in the forest.

17

We knock at a peasant's door. The murderers look for us. I head for
Warsaw. I meet a man . . . They want to hand me over to the
police. I arrive in Warsaw.

At midnight we set off and leave the forest. The night is clear, and
we realize that we are not very far from . . . Treblinka. We roam
around, then return to the forest where we walk till morning.
On the way we come to a muddy stream. Our comrade Masaryk
crouches on all fours and drinks the muddy water. We do the same.

After three days of wandering, tired and hungry, we decide
that we have to take a chance and go to a peasant's house to find
out where we are and ask for something to eat.

I and my comrade Kalman, the one who set the gas chambers
on fire, knock at a peasant's gate. The others remain hidden in
the forest, afraid that we might encounter unfriendly people.

The peasant opens the gate but will not let us in. He tells us that Germans in automobiles and on bicycles have been looking for us all day long. At the same time we learn that the mayor has let it be known that any peasant who turns over a Jew to him or to the police will receive a big reward.

The peasant gives us a loaf of bread and some milk, asking for gold in exchange. We give him two watches. We learn that we are 15 kilometres from Treblinka. We want to find out if he knows where there are partisan units. He doesn't know, but he informs us that there are big forests 5 kilometres from here. We head in that direction and wander around for fourteen days. But we do not encounter any partisans. It often happens that when we knock at the gates of a peasant house, they refuse to open or to answer our questions. We are so weakened by hunger and thirst that we can hardly stand. We pull up potatoes and beets in the fields and eat them raw. Our situation is desperate. By day we are afraid to show ourselves since everyone we meet tells us that there are round-ups going on.

After a fortnight in the forests, seeing no way out, I propose that we take a chance and travel to Warsaw. Several of us have acquaintances there, and perhaps we will succeed in saving ourselves. My proposal is rejected out of fear that along the way we might fall into the hands of the murderers.

Seeing that it is impossible for me to remain, I decide to leave for Warsaw by myself. It is painful for me to take leave of my friends. Still, I start on my way. We embrace each other and express our wish that we may meet again.

After walking several kilometres I come to a village. It is evening. I enter a peasant's house. He is afraid to talk to me. He hands me a piece of bread and tells me that Warsaw is 99 kilometres away. As I stand there, I suddenly hear the sound of shooting in the distance. The peasant runs back into the house and shouts to me to run away at once. I run into the potato fields and hide there. I hear more shots. Night has fallen. Heavy rain begins to fall and continues all night. I lie there for twelve hours until dawn. I feel I will not be able get up, but with my last ounce of strength I get back on my feet. After walking a few kilometres, I see a man approaching me. By now indifferent to everything, I keep going. The man comes closer. I see from his clothes that he is a peasant and ask him the way. He thinks about it for a little while then asks me: – Are you one of those who fled Treblinka?

Seeing that he feels compassion for me, I tell him that I am indeed one of those who fled and ask him for help. He tells me that he has to go to the mill to buy flour for tomorrow's holiday. But he turns back with me towards his house, some 2 kilometres away. He leads the way and I follow.

When I enter his house I see a woman with a child in her arms. I embrace the little child and kiss it. The woman looks at me in astonishment and I tell her: – Dear lady, it is a whole year since I have seen a living child . . . The woman and I cry together. She gives me food, and, seeing that I am soaked through, she gives me a shirt of her husband's to put on. She mentions that it is her husband's last shirt.

I see that these people want to help me. Weeping, the woman says to me: – I would very much like to help you, but I am afraid of my neighbours. After all, I have a small child . . .

After spending half an hour with them, I thank them warmly and want to say goodbye. The peasant points through the window to a barn standing in the middle of the fields not far from us. The barn belongs to a rich peasant and no-one ever goes there. He advises me to hide there and come to him in the evenings, when he will give me food. I thank them and head for the barn. I burrow deep into the straw so that no-one can see me. A real stroke of luck.

When evening falls I crawl out of the straw and head for my friends' house. They receive me in a very friendly fashion. After I have been sitting there for a few minutes, a neighbour suddenly enters, and without so much as saying hello slaps me hard twice on the face. He screams: – Yid, come with me!

Unfortunately I am helpless. The woman, seeing what he means to do to me, begs him to let go of me and allow me to escape. But he refuses to budge. The woman kisses him and begs him: – Franek, what do you want with that man? Do you even know him?

He screams at her for defending me: – Don't you know that these bandits set fire to Treblinka? I'll get a reward for him!

Her entreaties and tears are in vain. Seeing that she cannot change his mind, she goes over to him, grabs him from behind and shouts to me to escape. I tear myself away and dash out of the house. I cross the garden and run a couple of hundred steps and lie down in the field. I decide not to run away since it would be a shame to lose such good people. When it is clear to me that Franek has gone, I crawl back towards my friends on all fours, go into the barn and lie down again. In the morning the peasant comes in and when he sees me he greets me warmly. He is afraid that I will be caught because the neighbours all around are very bad people. He brings me food several times a day, and in the evening I hide in the barn in the middle of the fields.

I spend about two weeks that way. Every evening I come to the house of these good people and they hand me food through the window. But then the owner of the barn arrives and unloads some grain there. I suspect that he has seen me and therefore decide to leave my hiding place for Warsaw come what may.

That evening I go to my friends and tell them of my decision. They try to dissuade me out of fear that I may fall into the hands of the police patrolling the roads. But I cannot be talked out of it and bid them goodbye. The peasant tells me that the nearest railway station is Kostki, about 7 kilometres away.

The trip is a difficult one, as the trains are full of police. Nevertheless I am able to get to Warsaw without incident, and thence to Piastów, where my friend Jarosz, a Pole, resides. At first he does not recognize me and tries to give me 5 zlotys. Then, when he realizes who I am, he is happy to see me and helps me with necessities. He also provides Aryan papers for me.

After spending several days with him, I break down physically and spiritually. I lose my appetite and am convinced that I have no right to be alive after all I have seen and experienced. My friends care for me and try to convince me that there are few witnesses left like me and that I need to live in order to tell it all.

Yes, I lived for a year in Treblinka under the most difficult conditions. After the revolt I wandered for two months, lived for a year as a Pole with false papers, then after the Warsaw Uprising I hid in a bunker for three and a half months until I was liberated on 17 January, 1945.

Yes, I remained alive and find myself among free people. But why, I often ask myself. Is it so that I might tell the world about the millions of innocent murdered victims, to be a witness to the innocent blood that was spilled by the hands of the murderers?

Yes, I remained alive to bear witness against the slaughterhouse of Treblinka!

THE HELL OF TREBLINKA

by Vasily Grossman

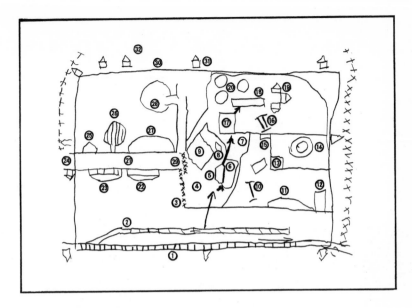

MAP DRAWN BY VASILY GROSSMAN IN SEPTEMBER 1944 WHILE WRITING "THE HELL OF TREBLINKA"

① RAILWAY LINE	⑰ "BATH HOUSE"
② BRANCH LINE CONSTRUCTED BY GERMANS	⑱ GRILL
③ BARBED-WIRE FENCE 6 METRES HIGH	⑲ BARRACKS FOR 300 JEWISH WORKERS
④ ROLL CALL SQUARE	⑳ GRAVE PITS
⑤ UNDRESSING	㉑ ROAD
⑥ WOMEN'S "HAIRDRESSERS"	㉒ ARSENAL
⑦ "ROAD OF NO RETURN"	㉓ BARRACKS FOR GERMAN STORES
⑧ LATRINE	㉔ GUARD HOUSE, 1 GERMAN, 5 UKRAINIANS
⑨ BARRACKS FOR JEWISH WORKERS, 700 MEN	㉕ ADMINISTRATION BUILDING
⑩ RECEPTION CAMP (LOWER CAMP)	㉖ "UKRAINIANS'" BARRACKS
⑪ CLOTHES STORE	㉗ BAKERY, DOCTOR, DENTIST, BARBER FOR GERMANS
⑫ SHOE STORE	㉘ ZOO
⑬ "DOCTOR'S HUT"	㉙ BARBED-WIRE FENCE 3 METRES HIGH
⑭ "LAZARET"	㉚ BARBED WIRE, PINE BRANCHES, BLANKETS, 3 METRES HIGH
⑮ LATRINE	㉛ WATCH TOWER, GUARD WITH MACHINE GUN
⑯ DEATH CAMP (UPPER CAMP)	㉜ ANTI-TANK BARRIER

THE BLACK ARROWS INDICATE THE PATH FOLLOWED BY A NEW TRANSPORT OF JEWS FROM ARRIVAL AT THE "STATION", THROUGH

THE UNDRESSING AREAS AND DOWN "THE ROAD OF NO RETURN" TO THE GAS CHAMBERS –

AND THEN THE GRILLS ON WHICH THE CORPSES WERE BURNED.

I

To the east of Warsaw, along the Western Bug, lie sands and swamps, and thick evergreen and deciduous forests. These places are gloomy and deserted; there are few villages. Travellers try to avoid the narrow roads, where walking is difficult and cartwheels sink up to the axle in the deep sand.

Here, on the branch line to Siedlce, stands the remote station of Treblinka. It is a little over sixty kilometres from Warsaw and not far from the junction station of Malkinia, where the lines from Warsaw, Białystok, Siedlce and Łomża all meet.

Many of those who were brought to Treblinka in 1942 may have had reason to pass this way in peaceful times. Gazing abstractedly at the dull landscape – pines, sand, sand and more pines, heather and dry shrubs, dismal station buildings and the intersections of tracks – bored passengers may have let their gaze settle for a moment on a single-track line running from the station into the middle of the dense pine forest around it. This spur led to a quarry where gravel was extracted for industrial and municipal construction projects.

This quarry is about four kilometres from the station, in a stretch of wilderness surrounded on all sides by pine forest. The soil here is poor and barren, and the peasants do not cultivate it. And so the wilderness has remained wilderness. The ground is partly covered by moss, with thin pines here and there. Now and then a jackdaw flies by, or a bright-coloured crested hoopoe. This miserable wilderness was the place chosen by some official, and approved by S.S. *Reichsführer* Himmler, for the construction of a vast executioner's block – an executioner's block such as the human race has never seen, from the time of primitive barbarism to our own cruel days. An executioner's block, probably, such as the entire universe has never seen. This was the site of the S.S.'s main killing ground, which surpassed those of Sobibór, Majdanek, Bełżec and Auschwitz.[1]

1   Bełżec and Auschwitz: The *Dictionnaire de la Shoah* gives an estimate of 900,000 deaths. Timothy Snyder, *Bloodlands* (New York: Basic Books, 2010, p. 408) gives a figure of 780,863 for the total number of Jews murdered at Treblinka. This is taken from a study by Peter Witte and Stephen Tyas ["A New Document on the Deportation and Murder of Jews during 'Einsatz Reinhard' 1942", *Holocaust and Genocide Studies*, vol. 15, no. 3, 2001, pp. 468–86]. Hershl Polyanker, a lesser-known Soviet journalist, gives the same mistaken estimate of three million deaths in an article written, like Grossman's, in September 1944. His "Treblinka – Hell on Earth", probably originally written in Yiddish, was translated into Spanish and sent by the Jewish Anti-Fascist Committee to newspapers in Cuba, Mexico and Uruguay [G.A.R.F., fond 8114 (Jewish Anti-Fascist Committee), opis' 1, delo 346, pp. 162–72].

There were two camps at Treblinka: Treblinka I, a penal camp for prisoners of various nationalities, chiefly Poles; and Treblinka II, the Jewish camp.

Treblinka I, a labour or penal camp, was located next to the quarry, not far from the edge of the forest. It was an ordinary camp, one of the hundreds and thousands of such camps that the Gestapo established in the occupied territories of Eastern Europe. It appeared in 1941. Many different traits of the German character, distorted by the terrible mirror of Hitler's regime, find expression in this camp. Thus the delirious ravings occasioned by fever are an ugly, distorted reflection of what the patient thought and felt before he was ill. Thus the acts and thoughts of a madman are a distorted reflection of the acts and thoughts of a normal person. Thus a criminal commits an act of violence; his hammer blow to the bridge of his victim's nose requires not only a sub-human cold-bloodedness but also the keen eye and firm grip of an experienced foundry worker.

Thrift, precision, calculation and pedantic cleanliness are qualities common to many Germans, and they are not bad qualities in themselves. They yield valuable results when applied to agriculture or industry. Hitler's regime, however, harnessed these qualities for a crime against humanity. In this Polish labour camp the S.S. acted as if they were doing something no more out of the ordinary than growing cauliflowers or potatoes.

The camp was laid out in neat uniform rectangles; the barracks were built in straight rows; birch trees lined the sand-covered paths. Asters and dahlias grew in the fertilized soil. There were concrete ponds for the ducks and geese; there were small pools, with convenient steps, where the staff could do their laundry. There were services for the German personnel: an excellent bakery, a barber's, a garage, a petrol pump with a glass ball on top, stores. The Majdanek camp outside Lublin was organized along the same principles – as were dozens of other labour camps in eastern Poland where the S.S. and the Gestapo intended to settle in for a long time; there were the same little gardens, the same drinking fountains, the same concrete roads. Efficiency, precise calculation, a pedantic concern for order, a love of detailed charts and schedules – all these German qualities were reflected in the layout and organization of these camps.

People were sent to the labour camp for various periods of time, sometimes as little as four to six months. There were Poles who had infringed the laws of the General Government – usually this was a matter of minor infringements, since the penalty for major infringements was immediate death. A slip of the tongue, a word overheard on the street, a failure to make some delivery, someone else's random denunciation, a refusal to hand over a cart or a horse to a German, a young girl being so bold as to refuse the advances of a member of the S.S., the merest unproven hint of suspicion of being involved in some act of sabotage at a factory, these were the offences that brought thousands of Polish workers, peasants and intellectuals – the old and the young, mothers, men and young girls – to this penal camp. Altogether, about fifty thousand people passed through its gates. Jews ended up in this camp only if they were unusually skilled craftsmen: bakers, cobblers, cabinet-makers, stonemasons, tailors. There were all kinds of work-shops in the camp, including a substantial furniture workshop that supplied the headquarters of German armies with tables, upright chairs and armchairs.

Treblinka I existed from the autumn of 1941 until 23 July, 1944. By the time it had been fully destroyed, the prisoners could already hear the distant rumble of Soviet artillery. Early in the morning of 23 July, the S.S. men and the *Wachmänner* fortified themselves with a stiff schnapps and set to work to wipe out every last trace of the camp. By nightfall all the prisoners had been killed and buried. Max Levit, a Warsaw carpenter, managed to survive; he lay wounded beneath the corpses of his comrades until it grew dark, and then he crawled off into the forest. He told us how, as he lay in the pit, he heard thirty boys from the camp singing "Broad is my Motherland!" just before they were shot. He heard one of the boys shout, "Stalin will avenge us!" He told us how the red-headed Leib – one of the most popular of the pris-oners and the leader of this group of boys – fell down on top of him after the first volley, raised his head a little and called out, "*Panie Wachman*, you didn't kill me. Shoot again, please! Shoot again!"

It is now possible to describe the regime of this labour camp in some detail; we have testimonies from dozens of Polish men and women who escaped or were released at one time or another. We know about work in the quarry; we know how those who failed to fulfil their work norm were thrown over the edge of a cliff into an abyss below. We know about the daily food ration: 170–200 grams of bread and half a litre of some slop that passed for soup. We know about the deaths from starvation, about the hunger-swollen wretches who were taken outside the camp in wheel-barrows and shot. We know about the wild orgies; we know how the Germans raped young women and shot them immediately afterwards. We know how people were thrown from a window six metres high. We know that a group of drunken Germans would sometimes take ten or fifteen prisoners from a barrack at night and calmly demonstrate different killing methods on them, shooting them in the heart, the back of the neck, the eyes, the mouth and the temple. We know the names of the S.S. men in the camp; we know their characters and idiosyncracies. We know that the head of the camp was a Dutch German named van Euppen, an insatiable murderer and sexual pervert with a passion for good horses and fast riding. We know about a huge young man named Stumpfe who broke out into uncontrollable laughter every time he murdered a prisoner or when one was executed in his presence. He was known as "Laughing Death". The last person to hear him laugh was Max Levit, on 23 July of this year, when thirty boys were shot on Stumpfe's orders and Levit was lying at the bottom of the pit. We know about Svidersky, a one-eyed German from Odessa who was known as "Master Hammer" because of his supreme expertise in "cold murder", i.e. killing without firearms. It took him only a few minutes – with no weapon but a hammer – to kill fifteen children, aged eight to thirteen, who had been declared unfit for work. We know about Preifi, a skinny S.S. man who looked like a Gypsy and whose nickname was "The Old One". He was sullen and taciturn. He would relieve his melancholy by sitting on the camp rubbish dump and waiting for a prisoner to sneak up in search of potato peelings; he would then shoot the prisoner in the mouth, having forced him or her to hold their mouth open.

We know the names of the professional killers Schwarz and Ledeke. They used to amuse themselves by shooting at prisoners returning from work in the twilight. They killed twenty, thirty or forty every evening.

None of these beings was in any way human. Their distorted brains, hearts and souls, their words, acts and habits were like a caricature – a terrible caricature of the qualities, thoughts, feelings, habits and acts of normal Germans. The orderliness of the camp; the documentation of the murders; the love of monstrous practical jokes that recall the jokes of drunken German students; the sentimental songs that the guards sang in unison amid pools of blood; the speeches they were constantly delivering to their victims; the exhortations and pious sayings printed neatly on special pieces of paper – all these monstrous dragons and reptiles were the progeny of traditional German chauvinism. They had sprung from arrogance, conceit and egotism, from a pedantic obsession with one's own little nest, from a steely indifference to the fate of everything living, from a ferocious, blind conviction that German science, German music, poetry, language, lawns, toilets, skies, beer and homes were the finest in the entire universe. These people's vices and crimes were born of the vices of the German national character, and of the German State.

Such was life in this camp, which was like a lesser Majdanek, and one might have thought that nothing in the world could be more terrible. But those who lived in Treblinka I knew very well that there was indeed something more terrible – a hundred times more terrible – than this camp. In May 1942, three kilometres away from the labour camp, the Germans had begun the construction of a Jewish camp, a camp that was, in effect, one vast executioner's block. Construction proceeded rapidly, with more than a thousand workers involved. Nothing in this camp was adapted for life; everything was adapted for death. Himmler intended the existence of this camp to remain a profound secret; not a single person was to leave it alive. And not a single person – not even a field marshal – was allowed near it. Anyone who happened to come within a kilometre of the camp was shot without warning. German planes were forbidden to fly over the area. The victims brought by train along the spur from Treblinka village did not know what lay in wait for them until the very last moment. The guards who had accompanied the prisoners during the journey were not allowed into the camp; they were not allowed even to cross its outer perimeter. When the trains arrived, S.S. men took over from the previous guards. The trains, which were usually made up of sixty freight wagons, were divided into three sections while they were still in the forest, and the locomotive would push twenty wagons at a time up to the camp platform. The locomotive always pushed from behind and stopped by the perimeter fence, and so neither the driver nor the fireman ever crossed the camp boundary. When the wagons had been unloaded, the S.S. *Unteroffizier* on duty would signal for the next twenty wagons, which would be waiting two hundred metres down the line. When all sixty wagons had been fully unloaded, the camp *Kommandantur* would phone the station to say they were ready for the next transport. The empty train then went on to the quarry, where the wagons were loaded with gravel before returning to Treblinka and then on to Małkinia.

Treblinka was well located; it was possible to bring transports from all four points of the compass: north, south, east and west. Trains came from the Polish cities of Warsaw, Międzyrzecz, Częstochowa, Siedlce and Radom; from Łomża, Białystok, Grodno and other Belorussian cities; from Germany, Czechoslovakia and Austria; and from Bulgaria and Bessarabia.

Every day for thirteen months the trains brought people to the camp. In each train there were sixty wagons, and a number chalked on the side of each wagon – 150, 180, 200 – indicated the number of people inside. Railway workers and peasants secretly kept count of these trains. Kazimierz Skarzuński, a sixty-two-year-old peasant from the village of Wólka (the nearest inhabited point to the camp), told me that there were days when as many as six trains went by from Siedlce alone, and that there was barely a day during these thirteen months without at least one train. And the line from Siedlce was only one of the four lines that supplied the camp. Lucjan Żukowa, who was enlisted by the Germans to work on the spur from Treblinka village, said that throughout the time he worked on this line, from 15 June, 1942 until August 1943, one to three trains went to the camp each day. There were sixty wagons in each train, and at least 150 people in each wagon. We have collected dozens of similar testimonies. Even if we were to halve the figures provided by these observers, we would still find that around two-and-a-half to three million people were brought to Treblinka during these thirteen months. We shall, however, return to this figure.

The fenced-off area of the camp proper, including the station platform, storerooms for the executed people's belongings and other auxiliary premises, is extremely small: 780 by 600 metres. If for a moment one were to entertain the least doubt as to the fate of the millions transported here, if one were to suppose for a moment that the Germans did not murder them immediately after their arrival, then one would have to ask what has happened to them all. There were, after all, enough of them to populate a small State or a large European capital. The area of the camp is so small that, had the new arrivals stayed alive for even a few days, it would have been only a week and a half before there was no more space behind the barbed wire for this tide of people flowing in from Poland, from Belorussia, from the whole of Europe. For thirteen months – 396 days – the trains left either empty or loaded with gravel. Not a single person brought by train to Treblinka II ever made the return journey. The terrible question has to be asked: "Cain, where are they? Where are the people you brought here?"

Fascism did not succeed in concealing its greatest crime – but this is not simply because there were thousands of involuntary witnesses to it. It was during the summer of 1942 that Hitler took the decision to exterminate millions of innocent people; the *Wehrmacht* was enjoying its greatest successes and Hitler was confident that he could act with impunity. We can see now that it was during this year that the Germans carried out their greatest number of murders. Certain that they would escape punishment, the Fascists showed what they were capable of. And had Hitler won, he would have succeeded in covering up every trace of his crimes. He would have forced every witness to keep silent. Even had there been not just thousands but tens of thousands of witnesses, not one would have said a word. And once again one cannot but pay homage to the men who – at a time of universal silence, when a world now so full of the clamour of victory was saying not a word – battled on in Stalingrad, by the steep bank of the Volga, against a German army to the rear of which lay gurgling, smoking rivers of innocent blood. It is the Red Army that stopped Himmler from keeping the secret of Treblinka.

Today the witnesses have spoken; the stones and the earth have cried out aloud. And today, before the eyes of humanity, before the conscience of the whole world, we can walk step by step around each circle of the Hell of Treblinka, in comparison with which Dante's Hell seems no more than an innocent game on the part of Satan.

Everything written below has been compiled from the accounts of living witnesses; from the testimony of people who worked in Treblinka from the first day of the camp's existence until 2 August, 1943, when the condemned rose up, burnt down the camp and escaped into the forest; from the testimony of *Wachmänner* who have been taken prisoner and who have confirmed the witnesses' accounts and often filled in the gaps. I have seen these people myself and have heard their stories, and their written testimonies lie on my desk before me. These many testimonies from a variety of sources are consistent in every detail – from the habits of Barry, the commandant's dog, to the technology used for the conveyor-belt executioner's block.

Let us walk through the circles of the Hell of Treblinka.

Who were the people brought here in trainloads? For the main part, Jews. Also some Poles and Gypsies. By the spring of 1942 almost the entire Jewish population of Poland, Germany and the western regions of Belorussia had been rounded up into ghettoes. Millions of Jewish people – workers, craftsmen, doctors, professors, architects, engineers, teachers, artists and members of other professions, together with their wives, daughters, sons, mothers and fathers – had been rounded up into the ghettoes of Warsaw, Radom, Częstochowa, Lublin, Białystok, Grodno and dozens of smaller towns. In the Warsaw ghetto alone there were around half a million Jews. Confinement to the ghetto was evidently the first, preparatory stage of Hitler's plan for the extermination of the Jews.

The summer of 1942, the time of Fascism's greatest military success, was chosen as the time to put into effect the second stage of this plan: physical extermination. We know that Himmler came to Warsaw at this time and issued the necessary orders. Work on the construction of the vast executioner's block proceeded day and night. By July the first transports were already on their way to Treblinka from Warsaw and Częstochowa. People were told that they were being taken to the Ukraine, to work on farms there; they were allowed to take food and twenty kilograms of luggage. In many cases the Germans forced their victims to buy train tickets for the station of "Ober-Majdan", a code word for Treblinka. Rumours about Treblinka had quickly spread through the whole of Poland, and so the S.S. had to stop using the name when they were herding people on to the transports. Nevertheless, people were treated in such a way as to be left with little doubt about what lay in store for them. At least 150 people, but more often 180 to 200, were crowded into each freight wagon. Throughout the journey, which sometimes lasted two or three days, they were given nothing to drink. People's thirst was so terrible that they would drink their own urine. The guards would offer a mouthful of water for a hundred zloty, but they usually just pocketed the money. People were packed so tightly together that sometimes they only had room to stand. In each wagon, especially during the stifling days of summer, a number of the old or those with weak hearts would die. Since the doors were kept shut throughout the journey, the corpses would begin to decompose, poisoning the air inside. And someone had only to light a match during the night for guards to start shooting through the walls. A barber by the name of Abram Kon states that in his wagon alone five people died as a result of such incidents, and a large number of people were wounded.

The conditions on the trains arriving from Western Europe were very different. The people in these trains had never heard of Treblinka, and they believed until the last minute that they were being taken somewhere to work. The Germans told them charming stories of the pleasures and comforts of the new life awaiting them once they had been resettled. Some trains brought people who were convinced that they were being taken to a neutral country; they had, after all, paid the German authorities large sums of money for the necessary visas.

Once a train arrived in Treblinka bringing citizens of Canada, America and Australia who had been stranded in Western Europe and Poland when the war broke out. After prolonged negotiations and the payment of huge bribes, they were allowed to travel to neutral countries. All the trains from Western Europe were without guards; they had the usual staff, along with sleeping and dining cars. The passengers brought large trunks and cases, as well as ample supplies of food. When trains stopped at stations, children would run out and ask how much further it was to Ober-Majdan.

There were a few transports of Gypsies from Bessarabia and elsewhere. There were also a number of transports of young Polish workers and peasants who had taken part in uprisings or joined partisan units.

It is hard to say which is the more terrible: to go to your death in agony, knowing that the end is near, or to be glancing unsuspectingly out of the window of a comfortable coach just as someone from Treblinka village is phoning the camp with details of your recently arrived train and the number of people on it.

In order to maintain until the very end the deception of the Western European passengers, the railhead at the death camp was got up to look like an ordinary railway station. On the platform where a batch of twenty carriages was being unloaded stood what seemed like a station building with a ticket office, a left-luggage office and a restaurant. There were arrows everywhere, with signs reading "To Białystok", "To Baranowicze", "To Wojkowice", etc. An orchestra played in the station building to greet the new arrivals, and the musicians were well dressed. A station guard in railway uniform collected tickets and let the passengers through on to a large square.

Soon the square would be filled by three to four thousand people, laden with bags and suitcases. Some were supporting the old and the sick. Mothers were holding little children in their arms; older children clung to their parents as they looked around inquisitively. There was something sinister and terrifying about this square that had been trodden by millions of human feet. People's sharp eyes were quick to notice alarming little signs. Lying here and there on the ground – which had evidently been swept only a few minutes before their arrival – were all kinds of abandoned objects: a bundle of clothing, some open suitcases, a few shaving brushes, some enamelled saucepans. How had they got there? And why did the railway line end just beyond the station? Why was there only yellow grass and three-metre-high barbed wire? Where were the lines to Białystok, Siedlce, Warsaw and Wojkowice? And why was there such an odd smile on the faces of the new guards as they looked at the men adjusting their ties, at the respectable old ladies, at the boys in sailor suits, at the slim young girls still managing to look neat and tidy after the journey, at the young mothers lovingly adjusting the blankets wrapped around babies who were wrinkling their little faces?

All these *Wachmänner* in black uniforms and S.S. *Unteroffiziere* were similar, in their behaviour and psychology, to cattle drivers at the entrance to a slaughterhouse. The S.S. and the *Wachmänner* did not see the newly-arrived transport as being made up of living human beings, and they could not help smiling at the sight of manifestations of embarrassment, love, fear and concern for the safety of loved ones or possessions. It amused them to see mothers straightening their children's jackets or scolding them for running a few yards away, to see men wiping their brows with a handkerchief and then lighting a cigarette, to see young girls tidying their hair, looking in pocket mirrors and anxiously holding down their skirts if there was a gust of wind. They thought it funny that the old men should try to squat down on their little suitcases, that some should be carrying books under their arms, that the sick should moan and groan and have scarves tied around their necks.

Up to twenty thousand people passed through Treblinka every day. Days when only six or seven thousand people passed through the station building were considered quiet. The square would fill with people four or five times each day. And all these thousands, all these tens and hundreds of thousands of people, of frightened, questioning eyes, all these young and old faces, all these dark- and fair-haired beauties, these bald and hunch-backed old men and these timid adolescents – all were caught up in a single flood, a flood that swallowed up reason, and splendid human science, and maidenly love, and childish wonder, and the coughing of the old, and the human heart.

And the new arrivals trembled as they sensed the strangeness of the look on the faces of the watching *Wachmänner* – a cool, sated, mocking look, the look of superiority with which a living beast surveys a dead human being.

And once again during these brief moments the people who had come out into the square found themselves noticing all kinds of alarming and incomprehensible trifles.

What lay behind that huge six-metre-high wall covered with blankets and yellowing pine branches? Even the blankets were somehow frightening. Quilted, many-coloured, silken or with calico covers, they looked all too similar to the blankets the newcomers had brought with them. How had these blankets got here? Who had brought them? And who were their owners? And why didn't they need their blankets any longer? And who were these men wearing light-blue armbands? Troubling suspicions came back to mind, frightening rumours that had been passed on in a whisper. But no, no, this was impossible. And the terrible thought was dismissed.

This sense of alarm always lasted a little while, perhaps two or three minutes, until everyone had made their way to the square. There was always a slight delay at this point; there were always cripples, the old, the sick and the lame, people who could barely move their legs. But soon everybody was present.

An S.S. *Unteroffizier* instructs the newcomers in a loud, clear voice to leave their things in the square and make their way to the bathhouse, taking with them only identity documents, valuables and toiletries. They want to ask all kinds of questions: should they take their underwear? Is it really alright to undo their bundles? Aren't all their belongings going to get mixed up? Might they not disappear altogether? But some strange force makes them hurry on in silence, not looking back, not asking questions, towards an opening – an opening in a barbed-wire wall, six metres high, that has been threaded with branches. They walk past anti-tank hedgehogs, past thickets of barbed wire three times the height of a human being, past an anti-tank ditch three metres deep, past thin coils of steel wire strewn on the ground to trip a fugitive and catch him like a fly in a spider's web, past another wall of barbed wire many metres high. And everyone is overwhelmed by a sense of helplessness, a sense of doom. There is no way to escape, no way to turn back, no way to fight back: staring down at them from low squat wooden towers are the muzzles of heavy machine guns. Should they call out for help? But all around them are S.S. men and *Wachmänner* armed with sub-machine guns, hand grenades and pistols. These men are power; they are power itself. Tanks, aircraft, lands, cities and sky, railways, the law, newspapers, radio – everything is in their hands. The whole world is silent, crushed, enslaved by a gang of bandits who have seized all power. London is silent, and so is New York. And only somewhere thousands of kilometres distant, on the banks of the Volga, is the Soviet artillery pounding away, obstinately proclaiming the determination of the Russian people to fight to the death for liberty, calling upon every nation to join in the battle.

Back on the square by the station two hundred workers with light-blue armbands ("the blue squad") were silently, swiftly and deftly untying bundles, opening baskets and suitcases, removing straps from bedrolls. The belongings of the new arrivals are being sorted out and appraised. On to the ground tumble neatly packed darning kits, spools of thread, children's underwear, shirts, sheets, pullovers, little knives, shaving kits, bundles of letters, photographs, thimbles, scent bottles, mirrors, bonnets, shoes, home-made boots made from quilted blankets (to protect against extreme cold), ladies' slippers, stockings, lace, pyjamas, packs of butter, coffee, tins of cocoa, prayer shawls, candlesticks, books, dry biscuits, violins, children's toy building blocks. It requires real skill to sort out, in the course of only a few minutes, all these thousands of objects. Everything of value is to be sent to Germany; everything old, shabby and valueless is to be burnt. And God help the unfortunate worker who puts an old wicker suitcase into a pile of leather cases destined for Germany, or who throws a new pair of stockings from Paris, still bearing their factory stamp, on to a heap of worn-out socks. Workers were not given the chance to make more than one mistake. Usually there were forty S.S. men and sixty *Wachmänner* "on transport duty", as they called this first stage of the work: meeting the trains, escorting people out from the "railway station" and into the square, and then supervising the workers with the light-blue armbands as they sorted through the things left behind on the square. These workers often infringed the regulations by slipping into their mouths little pieces of bread, sugar or sweets that they found. They were, however, allowed to wash their hands and faces with eau-de-cologne and perfume, given that there was a shortage of water at Treblinka and only *Wachmänner* and the S.S. were allowed to wash with it. And while the still-living people who had left all these things were preparing to enter the "bathhouse", the work of the blue squad was nearing completion. Items of value were already being taken away to the storerooms, while the letters, the yellowed wedding announcements, the photographs of newborn babies, brothers and brides, all the thousands of little things that were so infinitely precious to their owners yet the merest trash to the masters of Treblinka were being gathered into heaps and taken away to vast pits already containing hundreds of thousands of similar letters, postcards, visiting cards, photographs and sheets of paper covered in children's scribbles or children's first clumsy drawings in crayon. The square was then hurriedly swept and made ready to receive a new contingent of the doomed.

Not always, however, did things go so smoothly. Sometimes, when the prisoners knew where they were being taken, there were rebellions. Skrzeminski, a local peasant, twice saw people smash their way out of trains, knock down the guards and run for the forest. On both occasions every last person was killed by machine-gun fire. The men had been carrying four children, aged four to six; they too were shot. Another peasant, Marianna Kobus, has described similar attempts at escape. Once, when she was working in the fields, she saw sixty people break out of a train and run towards the forest; all were shot before her eyes.

But the contingent of new arrivals has now reached a second square, inside the inner camp fence. On one side of this square stands a single huge barrack, and there are three more barracks to the right. Two of these are used for storing clothes, the third for storing footwear. Further on, in the western section of the camp, are barracks for the S.S., barracks for the *Wachmänner*, food stores and a small farmyard. There are cars, trucks and an armoured vehicle. All in all, this seems like an ordinary camp, like Treblinka I.

In the south-eastern corner of the compound is an area fenced off with tree branches; towards the front of this area is a booth bearing the sign "Lazarett". The very old and the decrepit are separated from the crowd waiting for the "bathhouse" and taken on stretchers to this so-called infirmary. A man in a doctor's white coat, with a Red Cross armband on his left arm, comes out to meet them. Precisely what happened in the *Lazarett* – how the Germans used their Walther automatic pistols to spare old people from the burden of all possible diseases – I shall describe later.

The main thing in the next stage of processing the new arrivals was to break their will. There was a never-ending sequence of abrupt commands – bellowed out in a manner in which the German army takes pride, a manner that is proof in itself of the Germans being a master race. Simultaneously hard and guttural, the letter "r" sounded like the crack of a whip.

"*Achtung!*"

After this, in the leaden silence, the crowd would hear words that the *Scharführer* repeated several times a day for month after month: "Men are to remain where they are. Women and children must go to the barracks on the left and undress."

This, according to the accounts of eyewitnesses, marked the start of heart-rending scenes. Love – maternal, conjugal or filial love – told people that they were seeing one another for the last time. Handshakes, kisses, blessings, tears, brief hurried words into which people put all their love, all their pain, all their tenderness, all their despair . . . The S.S. psychiatrists of death knew that all this must be cut short, that these feelings must be stifled at once. The psychiatrists of death knew the simple laws that operate in slaughterhouses all over the world, laws which, in Treblinka, were exploited by brute beasts in order to deal with human beings. This was a critical moment: the moment when daughters were separated from fathers, mothers from sons, grandmothers from grandsons, husbands from wives.

Once again, echoing over the square: "*Achtung! Achtung!*" Once again people's minds must be confused with hope; once again the regulations of death must be passed off as the regulations of life. The same voice barks out word after word: "Women and children are to remove their footwear on entering the barrack. Stockings are to be put into shoes. The children's little stockings into their sandals, boots and shoes. Be tidy!"

And straight after this: "As you proceed to the bathhouse, take with you your valuables, documents, money, towel and soap. I repeat . . ."

Inside the women's barrack was a hairdresser's. The hair of the naked women was cut with clippers; old women had their wigs removed. This had a strange psychological effect: the hairdressers testify that this haircut of death did more than anything to convince the women that they really were going to the bathhouse. Young women would sometimes stroke their heads and say, "It's uneven here. Please make it smoother." Most of the women calmed down after their haircut; nearly all of them left the barrack carrying their piece of soap and a folded towel. Some young women wept over the loss of their beautiful plaits.

Why did the Germans shave women's hair? To deceive them better? No, Germany needed this hair. It was a raw material. I have asked many people what the Germans did with the hair that they removed from the heads of the living departed. Every witness said that the vast heaps of hair – black, red-gold and fair, straight, curly and wavy – were first disinfected, then packed into sacks and sent off to Germany. All the witnesses confirmed that the sacks bore German addresses. How was the hair used? No-one could answer. There is just one written deposition, from a certain Kohn, to the effect that the hair was used by the navy to fill mattresses and for such things as making hawsers for submarines. Other witnesses claim that the hair was used to pad saddles for the cavalry.

This testimony, in my view, requires further confirmation. In due course, this will be given to humanity by *Grossadmiral* Raeder, who in 1942 was in charge of the German Navy.

The men undressed outside, in the yard. One hundred and fifty to three hundred strong men from the first contingent of the day would be chosen to bury the corpses; they themselves were usually killed the following day. The men had to undress quickly but in an orderly manner, leaving their shoes, socks, underwear, jackets and trousers in neat piles. These were then sorted out by a second work squad, known as "the reds" because of the red armbands they wore to distinguish them from the squad "on transport duty". Items considered worth sending to Germany were taken to the store; first, though, any metal or cloth labels had to be carefully removed from them. All other items were burned or buried in pits.

Everyone was feeling more and more anxious. There was a terrible stench, intermingled with the smell of lime chloride. There were fat and persistent flies – an extraordinary number of them. What were they doing here, among pine-trees, on dry well-trodden ground? Everyone was breathing heavily now, shaking and trembling, staring at every little trifle that might give them some understanding, at anything that might lift the curtain of mystery and let them glimpse the fate that awaited them. And what were those gigantic excavators doing, rumbling away in the southern part of the camp?

Next, though, came another procedure. The naked people had to queue at a "ticket window" to hand over their documents and valuables. And again they heard that terrible, hypnotizing voice: "*Achtung! Achtung!*" The penalty for concealing valuables is death. "*Achtung! Achtung!*"

The *Scharführer* sat in a small wooden booth. Other S.S. men and *Wachmänner* stood nearby. On the ground were a number of wooden boxes into which they threw valuables. One was for paper money; one was for coins; a third was for watches, rings, earrings, and brooches with precious stones and bracelets. Documents were just thrown on the ground, since no-one had any use for the documents of the living dead who, within an hour, would be lying crushed in a pit. Gold and valuables, however, were carefully sorted; dozens of jewellers were engaged in ascertaining the quality of the metal, the value of the stones, the clarity of the diamonds.

Astonishingly, the brute beasts were able to make use of everything. Leather, paper, cloth – everything of use to man was of use to these beasts. It was only the most precious valuable in the world – human life – that they trampled beneath their boots. Powerful minds, honourable souls, glorious childish eyes, sweet faces of old women, proudly beautiful girlish heads that nature had toiled age after age to fashion – all this, in a vast silent flood, was condemned to the abyss of non-being. A few seconds was enough to destroy what nature and the world had slowly shaped in life's vast and tortuous creative process.

This booth with its small "ticket window" was a turning point. It marked the end of the process of torture by deception, the end of the lie that held people in a trance of ignorance, in a fever that hurled them between hope and despair, between visions of life and visions of death. This torture by deception aided the S.S. men in their work; it was an essential feature of the conveyor-belt executioner's block. Now, however, the final act had begun; the process of plundering the living dead was nearly completed, and the Germans changed their style of behaviour. They tore off rings and broke women's fingers; earlobes were ripped off along with earrings.

At this point a new principle had to be implemented if the conveyor-belt executioner's block was to continue to function smoothly. The word "*Achtung!*" was replaced by the hissing sounds of "*Schneller! Schneller! Schneller!* Faster! Faster! Faster! Faster into non-existence!"

We know from the cruel reality of recent years that a naked man immediately loses his powers of resistance. He ceases to struggle. Having lost his clothes, he loses his instinct of self-preservation and starts to accept whatever happens to him as his inevitable fate. Someone with an unquenchable thirst for life becomes passive and apathetic. Nevertheless, to make doubly sure that there were no mishaps, the S.S. found a way to stun their victims during this last stage of the conveyor belt's work, to reduce them to a state of complete psychic paralysis.

How did they achieve this?

Through a sudden recourse to pointless, alogical brutality. The naked people – people who had lost everything but who obstinately persisted in remaining human, a thousand times more so than the creatures around them wearing the uniforms of the German army – were still breathing, still looking, still thinking; their hearts were still beating. All of a sudden their towels and pieces of soap were knocked out of their hands. They were lined up in rows of five.

"*Hände hoch! Marsch! Schneller! Schneller!*"

They were then marched down a straight alley, 120 metres long and two metres wide, bordered by flowers and fir trees. This led to the place of execution. There was barbed wire on either side of the alley, which was lined by S.S. men and *Wachmänner* standing shoulder to shoulder, the former in grey uniforms, the latter in black. The path was sprinkled with white sand, and those who were walking in front with their hands in the air could see on this loose sand the fresh imprint of bare feet: the small footprints of women, the tiny footprints of children, the heavy footprints of the old. This faint trace in the sand was all that remained of the thousands of people who had not long ago passed this way, who had walked down this path just as the present contingent of four thousand people was now walking down it, just as another contingent of thousands, already waiting on the railway spur in the forest, would walk down it in two hours' time. Those whose footprints could be seen on the sand had walked down this path just as people had walked down it the day before, just as people had walked down it ten days before, just as people would walk down it the next day and in fifty days' time, just as people walked down it throughout the thirteen months of the existence of the Hell that was Treblinka.

The Germans referred to this alley as "The Road of No Return". A smirking, grimacing creature by the name of Suchomel used to shout out, deliberately garbling the German words: "Children, children, *schneller, schneller*, the water's getting cold in the bath-house! *Schneller*, children, *schneller!*" This creature would then burst out laughing; he would squat down and dance about. Hands above their heads, the people walked on in silence between the two rows of guards, who beat them with sticks, sub-machine-gun butts and rubber truncheons. The children had to run to keep up with the adults. Everyone who witnessed this last sorrowful procession has commented on the savagery of one particular member of the S.S.: Sepp. This creature specialized in the killing of children. Evidently endowed with unusual strength, it would suddenly snatch a child out of the crowd, swing him or her about like a cudgel and then either smash their head against the ground or simply tear them in half.

When I first heard about this creature – supposedly human, supposedly born of a woman – I could not believe the unthinkable things I was told. But when I heard these stories repeated by eye-witnesses, when I realized that these witnesses saw them as mere details, entirely in keeping with everything else about the hellish regime of Treblinka, then I came to believe that what I had heard was true.

Sepp's actions were necessary. They helped to reduce people to a state of psychic shock. They were an expression of the senseless cruelty that crushed both will and consciousness. He was a useful, necessary screw in the vast machine of the Fascist State.

What should appal us is not that nature gives birth to such monsters – there are, after all, any number of monsters in the physical world. There are Cyclops, and creatures with two heads, and there are corresponding psychic monstrosities and perversions. What is appalling is that creatures which should have been isolated and studied as psychiatric phenomena were allowed to live active lives, to be active citizens of a particular State. Their diseased ideology, their pathological psyches, their extraordinary crimes are, however, a necessary element of the Fascist State. Thousands, tens of thousands, hundreds of thousands of such creatures are pillars of German Fascism, the mainstay and foundation of Hitler's Germany. Dressed in uniforms and carrying weapons, decorated with imperial orders, these creatures lorded it for years over the peoples of Europe. It is not they that should appal us but the State that summoned them out of their holes, out of their underground darkness – the State that found them useful, necessary and even irreplaceable in Treblinka near Warsaw, in Majdanek near Lublin, in Bełżec, Sobibór and Auschwitz, in Babi Yar, in Domanevka and Bogdanovka near Odessa, in Trostyanets near Minsk, in Ponary in Lithuania and in hundreds of other prisons, labour camps, penal camps and camps for the destruction of life.

A particular kind of State does not appear out of nowhere. What engenders a particular regime are the material and ideological relations existing among a country's citizens. It is to these material and ideological relations that we need to devote serious thought; the nature of these relations is what should appal us.

The walk from the "ticket window" to the place of execution took only sixty to seventy seconds. Urged on by blows and deafened by shouts of "*Schneller! Schneller!*", the people came out into a third square and, for a moment, stopped in astonishment.

Before them stood a handsome stone building, decorated

with wooden fretwork and built in the style of an ancient temple. Five wide concrete steps led up to the low but very wide, massive, beautifully ornate doors. By the entrance there were flowers in large pots. Everything round about, however, was in chaos; everywhere you looked there were mountains of freshly dug earth. Grinding its steel jaws, a huge excavator was digging up tons of sandy yellow soil, raising a dust cloud that stood between the earth and the sun. The roar of the vast machine, which was digging mass graves from morning till night, mingled with the fierce barks of dozens of Alsatian dogs.

On either side of the house of death ran narrow-gauge tracks along which men in baggy overalls were pushing small self-tipping trolleys.

The wide doors of the house of death slowly opened, and in the entrance appeared two of the assistants to Schmidt, who was in charge of the complex. Both were sadists and maniacs. One, aged about thirty, was tall, with massive shoulders, black hair and a swarthy, laughing, animated face. The other, slightly younger, was short, with brown hair and pale yellow cheeks, as if he had just taken a strong dose of quinacrine. The names of these men who betrayed humanity, their motherland and their oaths of loyalty are known.

The tall man was holding a whip and a piece of heavy gas piping, about a metre long. The other man was holding a sabre.

Then the S.S. men would unleash their well-trained dogs, who would throw themselves into the crowd and tear with their teeth at the naked bodies of the doomed people. At the same time the S.S. men would beat people with submachine-gun butts, urging on petrified women with wild shouts of "*Schneller! Schneller!*"

Other assistants to Schmidt were inside the building, driving people through the wide-open doors of the chambers.

At this point Kurt Franz, one of the camp commandants, would appear, leading on a leash his dog Barry. He had specially trained this dog to leap up at the doomed people and tear out their sexual organs. Franz had done well for himself in the camp, starting as a junior S.S. *Unteroffizier* and attaining the fairly high rank of *Untersturmführer*. This tall, thin, thirty-five-year-old member of the S.S. was not only a gifted organizer who adored his work and could not imagine any better life for himself than his life at Treblinka, where nothing escaped his tireless vigilance – he was also something of a theoretician. He loved to explain the true significance of his work. Really, only one thing was missing during these last terrible moments by the doors of the chambers: the Pope himself, and Mr Brailsford, and other such humane defenders of Hitlerism, should have put in an appearance, in the capacity, it goes without saying, of spectators. Then they would have learned new arguments with which to enrich their humanitarian preachings, books and articles. And while he was about it, the Pope, who kept so reverently silent while Himmler was settling accounts with the human race, could have worked out how many batches his staff would have constituted, how long it would have taken the Treblinka S.S. to process the entire staff of his Vatican.

Great is the power of true humanity. Humanity does not die until man dies. And when we see a brief but terrifying period of history, a period during which beasts triumph over human beings, the man being killed by the beast retains to his last breath his strength of spirit, clarity of thought and passionate love. And the beast that triumphantly kills the man remains a beast. This immortality of spiritual strength is a sombre martyrdom – the triumph of a dying man over a living beast. It was this, during the darkest days of 1942, that brought about the beginning of reason's victory over bestial madness, the victory of good over evil, of light over darkness, of the forces of progress over the forces of reaction. A terrible dawn over a field of blood and tears, over an ocean of suffering – a dawn breaking amid the cries of dying mothers and infants, amid the death rattles of the aged.

The beasts and the beasts' philosophy seemed to portend the sunset of Europe, the sunset of the world, but the red was not the red of a sunset, it was the red blood of humanity – a humanity that was dying yet achieving victory through its death. People remained people. They did not accept the morality and laws of Fascism. They fought it in all ways they could; they fought it by dying as human beings.

To hear how the living dead of Treblinka preserved until the last moment not only the image and likeness of human beings but also the souls of human beings is to be shaken to one's very core; it is to be unable to find sleep or any peace of mind. We heard stories of women trying to save their sons and thus accomplishing feats of hopeless bravery. We heard of women trying to hide their little babies in heaps of blankets and trying to shield them with their own bodies. Nobody knows, and nobody ever will know, the names of these mothers. We heard of ten-year-old girls comforting their sobbing parents with divine wisdom; we heard of a young boy shouting out by the entrance to the gas chamber, "Don't cry, Mama – the Russians will avenge us!" Nobody knows, and nobody ever will know, what these children were called. We heard about dozens of doomed people, fighting alone against a band of S.S. men armed with machine guns and hand grenades – and dying on their feet, their breasts riddled with bullets. We heard about a young man stabbing an S.S. officer, about a youth who had taken part in the uprising in the Warsaw Ghetto and who by some miracle managed to hide a hand grenade from the Germans; already naked, he threw it into a group of executioners. We heard about a battle that lasted all through the night between a group of the doomed and units of S.S. and *Wachmänner*. All night long there were shots and explosions – and when the sun rose next morning, the whole square was covered with the fighters' bodies. Beside each lay a weapon: a knife, a razor, a stake torn from a fence. However long the earth lasts, we will never know the names of the fallen. We heard about a tall young woman who, on "The Road of No Return", tore a carbine from the hands of a *Wachmann* and fought back against dozens of S.S. Two of the beasts were killed in this struggle, and a third had his hand shattered. He returned to Treblinka with only one arm. She was subjected to terrible tortures and to a terrible execution. No-one knows her name; no-one can honour it.

Yet is that really so? Hitlerism took from these people their homes and their lives; it wanted to erase their names from the world's memory. But all of them – the mothers who tried to shield their children with their own bodies, the children who wiped away the tears in their fathers' eyes, those who fought with knives and flung hand grenades, and the naked young woman who, like a goddess from a Greek myth, fought alone against dozens – all these people, though they are no longer among the living, have preserved for ever the very finest name of all, a name that no pack of Hitlers and Himmlers has been able to trample into the ground, the name: Human Being. The epitaph History will write for them is "Here Lies a Human Being".

The inhabitants of Wólka, the nearest village to the camp, say that there were occasions when they could not endure the screams of the women being killed. They would all disappear deep into the forest – anything not to hear those screams that penetrated wooden walls, that pierced the earth and the sky. Sometimes the screams would suddenly fall silent, only to break out again equally suddenly, as all-penetrating as before, piercing bones, boring through skulls and souls . . . And this was repeated three or four times a day.

I questioned one of the executioners whom we had taken prisoner. He explained that the women began to scream when the dogs were set on them and the entire contingent of doomed people was being driven into the house of death: "They could see death. Besides, it was very crowded in there, and the dogs were tearing at them, and they were being badly beaten by the *Wachmänner*."

The sudden silence was when the doors of the gas chamber were closed. And the screams began again when a new contingent was brought there. This was repeated three, four, sometimes five times each day. After all, the Treblinka executioner's block was no ordinary executioner's block. It was a conveyor-belt executioner's block; it was run according to the same principles as any other large-scale modern industrial enterprise.

Like any other industrial enterprise, Treblinka grew gradually, developing and acquiring new production areas; it was not always as I have described it above. In the beginning there were three small gas chambers. While these were still under construction, a number of transports arrived, and the people they brought were murdered with "cold" weapons: axes, hammers and clubs. The Germans did not want to use guns, since this would have revealed the true purpose of Treblinka to the surrounding population. The first three concrete chambers were relatively small, five metres by five metres and 190 centimetres high. Each chamber had two doors: one through which the living were admitted, one through which the corpses of the gassed were dragged out. The second door was very wide, about 2.5 metres. The three chambers stood side by side on a single foundation.

These three chambers lacked capacity; they could not generate the conveyor-belt power required by Berlin.

The construction of a larger building was begun straightaway. The officials in charge of Treblinka took pride and joy in the fact that, in terms of power, handling capacity and production floor space, this would far surpass the other S.S. death factories: Majdanek, Sobibór and Bełżec.

Seven hundred prisoners worked for five weeks on the construction of the new death facility. When the work was in full swing, an engineer arrived from Germany with a team of workers and began to install the equipment. The new gas chambers, ten in all, were symmetrically located on either side of a broad concrete corridor. Each chamber – like the three earlier chambers – had two doors: one from the corridor, for the admission of the living, the other in the opposite wall, so that the corpses of the gassed could be dragged out. These doors opened on to special platforms on either side of the building. Alongside these platforms were narrow-gauge tracks. The corpses were thrown out on to the platforms, loaded on to trolleys and then taken away to the mass graves that the vast excavators were digging day and night. The floor of each chamber sloped down from the central corridor towards the platform outside, and this greatly facilitated the work of unloading the chambers. In the earlier chambers the unloading methods had been primitive – the corpses had been carried out on stretchers or dragged out with the help of straps. Each new gas chamber was seven metres by eight metres. The floor area of the ten new chambers totalled 560 square metres. Including the three old chambers, which went on being used for smaller contingents, there was thus a total death-producing area of 635 square metres. From four hundred to six hundred people were loaded into each gas chamber; working at full capacity, the ten new chambers were therefore able to destroy four thousand to six thousand lives at once. The chambers of the Treblinka Hell were loaded at least two or three times a day (there were days when they were loaded six times). A conservative estimate indicates that a twice-daily operation of the new gas chambers alone would have meant the death of ten thousand people a day, three hundred thousand a month. Treblinka was functioning every day for thirteen months on end. But even if we allow ninety days for stoppages and repairs, and for delays on the railway, this still leaves us with ten months of uninterrupted operation. If the average number of deaths a month was three hundred thousand, then the number of deaths in ten months would have been three million. Once again we have come to the same figure: three million – the figure we arrived at before through a deliberately low estimate of the number of people brought to Treblinka by train. We will return to this figure a third time.[2]

The death process in the gas chambers took from ten to twenty-five minutes. When the new chambers were first put into

---

2 Grossman is also mistaken with regard to the number of people killed during a single operation of the gas chambers. The true figure was probably between two thousand and three thousand.

operation and the executioners were still determining how best to administer the gas and which poisons to use, the victims sometimes remained alive for two to three hours, undergoing terrible agony. During the very first days there were serious problems with the delivery and exhaust systems, and the victims were in torment for anything up to nine or ten hours. Various means were employed to effect death. One was to force into the chambers the exhaust fumes from the engine, taken from a heavy tank, that was used to generate electricity for the camp. Such fumes contain 2 to 3 per cent of carbon monoxide, which combines with the haemoglobin in the blood to form a stable compound known as carboxyhaemoglobin. Carboxyhaemoglobin is far more stable than the compound of oxygen and haemoglobin that is formed in the alveoli during the respiratory process. Within fifteen minutes all the haemoglobin in the blood has combined with carbon monoxide, and breathing ceases to have any real effect. A person is gasping for air, but no oxygen reaches their organism and they begin to suffocate; the heart races frenziedly, driving blood into the lungs, but this blood, poisoned as it is with carbon monoxide, is unable to absorb any oxygen. Breathing becomes hoarse and laboured, and consciousness dims. People show all the agonizing symptoms of suffocation, and they die just as if they were being strangled.

A second method, and the one most generally employed at Treblinka, was the use of special pumps to remove the air from the chambers. As with the first method, death resulted from oxygen deprivation. A third method, employed less often, was the use of steam. This too brought about death from oxygen deprivation, since the steam had the effect of expelling the air from the chambers. Various poisons were also employed, but only on an experimental basis; it was the first and second of these methods that were employed for murder on an industrial scale.

The conveyor belt of Treblinka functioned in such a way that beasts were able methodically to deprive human beings of everything to which they have been entitled, since the beginning of time, by the holy law of life.

First people were robbed of their freedom, their home and their motherland; they were transported to a nameless wilderness in the forest. Then, on the square by the station, they were robbed of their belongings, of their personal letters, and of photographs of their loved ones. After going through the fence, a man was robbed of his mother, his wife and his child. After he had been stripped naked, his papers were thrown on to a fire; he had been robbed of his name. He was driven into a corridor with a low stone ceiling; now he had been robbed of the sky, the stars, the wind and the sun.

Then came the last act of the human tragedy – a human being was now in the last circle of the Hell that was Treblinka.

The door of the concrete chamber slammed shut. The door was secured by every possible kind of fastening: by locks, by hooks, by a massive bolt. It was not a door that could be broken down.

Can we find within us the strength to imagine what the people in these chambers felt, what they experienced during their last minutes of life? All we know is that they cannot speak now . . . Covered by a last clammy mortal sweat, packed so tight that their bones cracked and their crushed ribcages were barely able to breathe, they stood pressed against one another; they stood as if they were a single human being. Someone, perhaps some wise old man, makes the effort to say, "Patience now – this is the end." Someone shouts out some terrible curse. A holy curse – surely this curse must be fulfilled? With a superhuman effort a mother tries to make a little more space for her child: may her child's dying breaths be eased, however infinitesimally, by a last act of maternal care. A young woman, her tongue going numb, asks, "Why am I being suffocated? Why can't I love and have children?" Heads spin. Throats choke. What are the pictures now passing before people's glassy dying eyes? Pictures of childhood? Of the happy days of peace? Of the last terrible journey? Of the mocking face of the S.S. man in that first square by the station: "Ah, so that's why he was laughing . . ." Consciousness dims. It is the moment of the last agony . . . No, what happened in that chamber cannot be imagined. The dead bodies stand there, gradually turning cold. It was the children, according to witnesses, who kept on breathing for longest. After twenty to twenty-five minutes Schmidt's assistants would glance through the peepholes. It was time to open the second doors, the doors to the platforms. Urged on by shouting S.S. men, prisoners in overalls set about unloading the chambers. Because of the sloping floor, many of the bodies simply tumbled out of their own accord. People who carried out this task have told me that the faces of the dead were very yellow and that around 70 per cent of them were bleeding slightly from the nose and mouth; physiologists, no doubt, can explain this.

S.S. men examined the bodies, talking to one another as they did so. If anyone turned out to be still alive, if anyone groaned or stirred, they were finished off with a pistol shot. Then a team of men armed with dental pliers would extract all the platinum and gold teeth from the mouths of the murdered people waiting to be loaded on to the trolleys. The teeth were then sorted according to value, packed into boxes and sent off to Germany. Had the S.S. found it in any way more convenient or advantageous to extract people's teeth while they were still alive, they would, of course, have done this without hesitation, just as they removed women's hair while they were still alive. But it was evidently easier and more convenient to extract people's teeth when they were dead.

The corpses were then loaded on to the trolleys and pushed along the narrow-gauge tracks towards long grave pits. There they were laid out in rows, packed closely together. The huge pit was not filled in; it was still waiting. In the meantime, as soon as the work of unloading the chambers had begun, the Scharführer "on transport duty" would have received a short order by telephone. The Scharführer would then blow his whistle – a signal to the engine driver – and another twenty wagons would be brought up slowly to the platform of a make-believe railway station called Ober-Majdan. Another three or four thousand people carrying suitcases, bundles and bags of food would get out and walk to the station square. Mothers were holding little children in their arms; elder children clung to their parents as they looked intently around. There was something sinister and terrifying about this square that had been trodden by millions of feet. And why did the railway line end just beyond the station? Why was there only yellow grass and three-metre-high barbed wire?

The processing of the new contingent was carefully timed; they set out along "The Road of No Return" just as the last corpses from the gas chambers were being taken towards the grave pits. The pit had not been filled in; it was still waiting.

A little later, the *Scharführer* would blow his whistle again – and another twenty wagons would slowly be brought up to the station platform. More thousands of people carrying suitcases, bundles and bags of food would get out and walk to the station square and look around. There was something sinister and terrifying about this square that had been trodden by millions of feet.

And the camp commandant, sitting in his office amid heaps of papers and charts, would telephone the station in Treblinka village – and another sixty-car train escorted by S.S. men with sub-machine guns and automatic rifles would pull heavily out of a siding and crawl along a single track between rows of pines.

The vast excavators worked day and night, digging vast new pits, pits that were many hundreds of metres long and many dark metres deep. And the pits were waiting. Waiting – though not for long.

2

As the winter of 1942–3 was drawing to an end, Himmler came to Treblinka, together with a group of important Gestapo officials. Himmler's party flew to a landing strip in the area and was then taken in two cars to the camp, which they entered by the main gate. Most of the visitors were in army uniform; some – perhaps the various scientific experts – seemed like civilians, in fur coats and hats. Himmler inspected the camp in person, and one of the people who saw him has told us that the minister of death walked up to a huge grave pit and, for a long time, stared silently into it. His retinue waited at a respectful distance as Heinrich Himmler contemplated the colossal grave, already half full of corpses. Treblinka was the most important of all the factories in Himmler's empire. Later that same day the S.S. *Reichsführer* flew back. Before leaving Treblinka, he issued an order that dumbfounded the three members of the camp command: *Hauptsturmführer* Baron von Pfein, his deputy Karol and Captain Franz Stangl. They were to start work immediately on digging up the corpses and burning every last one of them; the ashes and cinders were to be removed from the camps and scattered over fields and roads. Since there were already millions of corpses in the ground, this would be an extraordinarily complex and difficult task. In addition, the newly gassed were to be burnt at once, instead of being buried.

What was the reason for Himmler's visit and his personal categorical order? The answer is very simple: the Red Army had just defeated the Germans at Stalingrad. This must have been a terrifying blow for the Germans. Within a matter of days men in Berlin were, for the first time, showing concern about being held to account, about possible retribution, about the revenge to which they might be subjected; within a matter of days Himmler himself had flown to Treblinka and issued urgent orders calculated to hide the traces of crimes committed within sixty kilometres of Warsaw. Himmler's orders were an echo, a direct repercussion of the mighty blow that the Red Army had just struck against the Germans, far away on the Volga.

At first there was real difficulty with the process of cremation; the corpses would not burn. There was, admittedly, an attempt to use the women's bodies, which burned better, to help burn the men's bodies. And the Germans tried dousing the bodies with petrol and fuel oil, but this was expensive and turned out to make only a slight difference. There seemed to be no way around this problem, but then a thickset man of about fifty arrived from Germany, a member of the S.S. and a master of his trade. Hitler's regime, after all, had the capacity to produce experts of all kinds: experts in the use of a hammer to murder small children, expert stranglers, expert designers of gas chambers, experts in the scientifically planned destruction of large cities in the course of a single day. The regime was also able to find an expert in the exhumation and cremation of millions of human corpses.

And so, under this man's direction, furnaces were constructed. Furnaces of a special kind, since neither the furnaces at Majdanek nor those of any of the largest crematoria in the world would have been able to burn so vast a number of corpses in so short a time.

The excavator dug a pit 250–300 metres long, 20–25 metres wide and 6 metres deep. Three rows of evenly spaced reinforced-concrete pillars, 100–120 centimetres in height, served as a support for giant steel beams that ran the entire length of the pit. Rails about five to seven centimetres apart were then laid across these beams. All this constituted a gigantic grill. A new narrow-gauge track was laid from the burial pits to the grill pit. Two more grill pits of the same dimensions were constructed soon afterwards; each took 3,500 to 4,000 corpses at once.

Another giant excavator arrived, soon followed by a third. The work continued day and night. People who took part in the work of burning the corpses say that these grill pits were like giant volcanoes. The heat seared the workers' faces. Flames erupted eight or ten metres into the air. Pillars of thick black greasy smoke reached up into the sky and stood there, heavy and motionless. At night, people from villages thirty or forty kilometres away could see these flames curling above the pine forest that surrounded the camp. The smell of burnt human flesh filled the whole area. If there was a wind, and if it blew in the direction of the labour camp three kilometres away, the people there almost suffocated from the stench. More than eight hundred prisoners – more than the number of workers employed in the furnaces of even the hugest of iron and steel plants – were engaged in the work of burning the bodies. This monstrous workshop operated day and night for eight months, without interruption, yet it still could not cope with the millions of human bodies. Trains were, of course, delivering new contingents to the gas chambers all the time, which added to the work of the grill pits.

Transports sometimes arrived from Bulgaria. These were a particular joy to the S.S. and the *Wachmänner*, since the Bulgarian Jews, who had been hoodwinked both by the Germans and by the Fascist Bulgarian government of the time, had no idea of the fate that awaited them and brought with them large quantities of valuables and plenty of tasty food, including white bread. Then there were transports from Grodno and Białystok, and – after the uprising – from the Warsaw Ghetto. There was a transport of rebels from other parts of Poland – peasants, workers and soldiers. There was a contingent of Bessarabian Gypsies: around two hundred men, with eight hundred women and children. They had come on foot, a string of horses and carts trailing behind them. They too had been hoodwinked; they were escorted by only two guards – and even these guards had no idea that they were leading these people to their death. I have been told that the Gypsy women clapped their hands in delight when they saw the handsome exterior of the gas chamber, and that they had no inkling until the very last minute of what lay in store for them. This greatly amused the Germans.

The S.S. singled out for particular torment those who had participated in the uprising in the Warsaw Ghetto. The women and children were taken not to the gas chambers but to where the corpses were being burned. Mothers crazed with horror were forced to lead their children on to the red-hot grid where thousands of dead bodies were writhing in the flames and smoke, where corpses tossed and turned as if they had come back to life again, where the bellies of women who had been pregnant burst from the heat and babies killed before birth were burning in open wombs. Such a spectacle was enough to rob the most hardened man of his reason, but its effect – as the Germans well knew – was a hundred times greater on a mother struggling to keep her children from seeing it. The children clung to their mothers and shrieked, "Mama, what are they going to do to us? Are they going to burn us?" Not even Dante, in his Hell, saw scenes like this.

After amusing themselves for a while with this spectacle, the Germans burned the children.

It is infinitely painful to read this. The reader must believe me when I say that it is equally hard to write it. "Why write about it then?" someone may well ask. "Why recall such things?"

It is the writer's duty to tell the terrible truth, and it is a reader's civic duty to learn this truth. To turn away, to close one's eyes and walk past is to insult the memory of those who have perished. Only those who have learned the whole truth can ever understand against what kind of monster our great and holy Red Army has entered into mortal combat.

The S.S. had begun to feel bored in Treblinka. The procession of the doomed to the gas chambers had ceased to excite them. It had become routine. When the cremation of the corpses began, the S.S. men spent hours by the grill pits; this new sight amused them. The expert who had just come from Germany used to stroll around between the grill pits from morning till night, always animated and talkative. People say they never saw him frown or even look serious; he was always smiling. When the corpses were thrown down on to the bars of the grill, he would repeat: "Innocent, innocent". This was his favourite word.

Sometimes the S.S. organized a kind of picnic by the grill pits; they would sit upwind from them, drink wine, eat and watch the flames. The "infirmary" was also re-equipped. During the first months the sick and the aged had been taken to a space screened off by branches – and murdered there by a so-called doctor. Their bodies had then been carried on stretchers to the mass graves. Now a round pit was dug. Around this pit, as if the infirmary were a stadium, was a circle of low benches, all so close to the edge that anyone sitting on them was almost dangling over the pit. On the bottom of the pit was a grill, and on it corpses were burning. After being carried into the "infirmary", sick and decrepit old people were taken by "nurses" to these benches and made to sit facing the bonfire of human bodies. After enjoying this sight for a while, the Nazi barbarians shot the old people in the back, or in the backs of their grey heads. Dead or wounded, the old people fell into the bonfire.

German humour has never been highly valued; we have all heard people speak of it as heavy-handed. But who on earth could have imagined the humour, the jokes, the entertainments of the S.S. at Treblinka? They organized football matches between teams of the doomed, they made the doomed play tag, they organized a choir of the doomed. A small zoo was set up near the Germans' sleeping quarters. Innocent beasts from the forest – wolves and foxes – were kept in cages, while the vilest and cruellest predators ever seen on earth walked about in freedom, sat down for a rest on little benches made of birch wood and listened to music. Someone even wrote a special anthem for the doomed, which included the words:

> Für uns giebt heute nur Treblinka,
>
> Das unser Schiksal ist . . .

A few minutes before their death, wounded, bleeding people were forced to learn idiotic and sentimental German songs and sing them in unison:

> . . . Ich brach das Blumelein
>
> Und schenkte es dem Schönste
>
> Geliebte Mädelein . . .

The chief commandant selected a few children from one contingent. He killed their parents, dressed the children up in fine clothes, gave them lots of sweets and played with them. A few days later, when he had had enough of this amusement, he gave orders for them to be killed.

The Germans posted one old man in a prayer shawl and phylacteries next to the outhouse and ordered him not to allow people to stay inside for more than three minutes. An alarm clock was hung from his chest. The Germans would look at his prayer shawl and laugh. Sometimes the Germans would force elderly Jewish men to recite prayers or to arrange funerals for those who had been murdered, observing all the traditional rites. They would even have to go and fetch gravestones – but after a while they were made to open the graves, dig up the bodies and destroy the gravestones.

One of the main entertainments was to rape and torment the beautiful young women whom the S.S. selected from each contingent. In the morning the rapists would personally accompany them to the gas chambers. Thus the S.S. – the bulwark of Hitler's regime and the pride of Fascist Germany – entertained themselves at Treblinka.

It needs to be emphasized that these creatures were far from being mere robots that mechanically carried out the wishes of their superiors. Every witness attests to their shared love of philosophizing. The S.S. loved to deliver speeches to the doomed; they loved to discuss what was happening at Treblinka and its profound significance for the future. They were all deeply and sincerely convinced that what they were doing was right and necessary. They explained at length how their race was superior to all other races; they delivered tirades about German blood, the German character and the mission of the German race. These beliefs have been expounded in books by Hitler and Rosenberg, in pamphlets and articles by Goebbels.

After they had finished work for the day, and after amusements such as those described above, they would sleep the sleep of the just, not disturbed by dreams or nightmares. They were not tormented by conscience, if only because not one of them possessed a conscience. They did gymnastics, drank milk every morning and generally took good care of their health. They showed no less concern with regard to their living conditions and personal comforts, surrounding their living quarters with tidy gardens, sumptuous flowerbeds and summerhouses. Several times a year they went on leave to Germany, since their bosses considered work in this "factory" detrimental to health and were determined to look after their workers. Back at home they walked about with their heads held high. If they said nothing about their work, this was not because they were ashamed of it but simply because, well disciplined as they were, they did not dare to violate their solemn pledge of silence. And when, in the evening, they went arm in arm with their wives to the cinema and burst into loud laughter, stamping their hobnailed boots on the floor, it would have been hard to tell them apart from the most ordinary man in the street. Nevertheless, they were beasts – vile beasts, S.S. beasts.

The summer of 1943 was exceptionally hot. For weeks on end there was no rain, no clouds and no wind. The work of burning the corpses was in full swing. Day and night for six months the grill pits had been blazing, but only a little more than half of the corpses had been burned.

The moral and physical torment began to tell on the prisoners charged with this task; every day fifteen to twenty prisoners committed suicide. Many sought death by deliberately infringing the regulations.

"To get a bullet was a luxury," I heard from a baker by the name of Kosów, who had escaped from the camp. In Treblinka, evidently, it was far more terrible to be doomed to live than to be doomed to die.

Cinders and ashes were taken outside the camp grounds. Peasants from the village of Wólka were ordered to load them on to their carts and scatter them along the road leading from the death camp to the labour camp. Child prisoners with spades then spread the ashes more evenly. Sometimes these children found melted gold coins or dental crowns. The ashes made the road black, like a mourning ribbon, and so the children were known as "the children from the black road". Car wheels make a peculiar swishing sound on this road, and, when I was taken along it, I kept hearing a sad whisper from beneath the wheels, like a timid complaint.

This black mourning-ribbon of ashes, lying between woods and fields, from the death camp to the labour camp, was like a tragic symbol of the terrible fate uniting the nations that had fallen beneath the axe of Hitler's Germany.

The peasants began carting out the cinders and ashes in spring 1943, and they continued until summer 1944. Each day twenty carts made from six to eight trips; during each trip they scattered 120 to 130 kilos of ash.

"Treblinka" – the song that eight hundred people were made to sing while they cremated corpses – included words exhorting the prisoners to humility and obedience; their reward would be "a little, little happiness, that would flash by in a single moment". Astonishingly, there really was one happy day in the living Hell of Treblinka. The Germans, however, were mistaken: what brought the condemned this gift was not humility and obedience. On the contrary, this happy day dawned thanks to insane audacity – thanks to the insane audacity of people who had nothing to lose. All were expecting to die, and every day of their life was a day of suffering and torment. All had witnessed terrible crimes, and the Germans would have spared none of them; the gas chambers awaited them all. Most, in fact, were sent to the gas chambers after only a few days of work, and were replaced by people from new contingents. Only a few dozen people lived for weeks and months, rather than for days and hours; these were skilled workers, carpenters and stonemasons, and the bakers, tailors and barbers who ministered to the Germans' everyday needs. These people created an Organizing Committee for an uprising. It was, of course, only the already-condemned, only people possessed by an all-consuming hatred and a fierce thirst for revenge, who could have conceived such an insane plan. They did not want to escape until they had destroyed Treblinka. And they destroyed it. Weapons – axes, knives and truncheons – began to appear in the prisoners' barracks. The risk they incurred, the price they paid to obtain each axe or knife, is hard to imagine. What cunning and skill, what astonishing patience, were required to hide these things in the barracks! Stocks of petrol were laid in – to douse the camp buildings and set them ablaze. How did the conspirators achieve this? How did petrol disappear, as if it had evaporated, from the camp stores? How indeed? Through superhuman effort – through great mental ingenuity, through determination and a terrifying audacity. A large tunnel was dug beneath the ammunition store. Audacity worked miracles; standing beside the conspirators was the God of courage. They took twenty hand grenades, a machine gun, rifles and pistols and hid them in secret places. Every detail in their complex plan was carefully worked out. Each group of five had its specific assignment. Each mathematically precise assignment called for insane daring. One group was to storm the watchtowers, where the *Wachmänner* sat with their machine guns. A second group was to attack the sentries who patrolled the paths between the various camp squares. A third group was to attack the armoured vehicles. A fourth was to cut the telephone lines. A fifth was to seize control of the barracks. A sixth would cut passages through the barbed wire. A seventh was to lay bridges across the anti-tank ditches. An eighth was to pour petrol on the camp buildings and set them on fire. A ninth group would destroy whatever else could be destroyed.

There were even arrangements to provide the escapees with money. There was one moment, however, when the Warsaw doctor who was collecting this money nearly ruined the whole plan. A *Scharführer* noticed a wad of banknotes sticking out of his pocket; the doctor had only just collected the notes and had been about to hide them away. The *Scharführer* pretended not to have seen anything and reported the matter to Kurt Franz. Something extraordinary was clearly going on – what use, after all, was money to a man condemned to death? – and Franz immediately went off to interrogate the doctor. He began the interrogation with calm confidence; there may well, after all, have been no more skilled torturer in the world. And there was certainly no-one at all in the world – Franz believed – who could withstand the tortures he practised. But the Warsaw doctor outwitted the S.S. *Hauptmann*. He took poison. One of the participants in the uprising told me that never before in Treblinka had such efforts been made to save a man's life. Evidently Franz sensed that the doctor would be slipping away with an important secret. But the German poison did its job, and the secret remained a secret.

Towards the end of June it turned suffocatingly hot. When graves were opened, steam billowed up from them as if from gigantic boilers. The heat of the grills – together with the monstrous stench – was killing even the workers who were moving the corpses; they were dropping dead on to the bars of the grills.

Billions of overfed flies were crawling along the ground and buzzing about in the air. The last hundred thousand corpses were now being burned.

The uprising was planned for 2 August. It began with a revolver shot. The banner of success fluttered over the holy cause. New flames soared into the sky – not the heavy flames and grease-laden smoke of burning corpses but bright wild flames of life. The camp buildings were ablaze, and to the rebels it seemed that a second sun was burning over Treblinka, that the sun had rent its body in two in celebration of the triumph of freedom and honour.

Shots rang out; machine-gun fire crackled from the watch-towers that the rebels had captured. Hand grenades rang out as triumphantly as if they were the bells of truth itself. The air shook from crashes and detonations; buildings collapsed; the buzzing of corpse flies was drowned out by the whistle of bullets. In the pure, clear air flashed axes red with blood. On 2 August the evil blood of the S.S. flowed on to the ground of the Hell that was Treblinka, and a radiant blue sky celebrated the moment of revenge. And a story as old as the world was repeated once more: creatures who had behaved as if they were representatives of a higher race; creatures who had shouted "*Achtung! Mützen ab!*" to make people take off their hats; creatures who had bellowed, in their masterful voices, "*Alle r-r-r-raus unter-r-r-r!*", to compel the inhabitants of Warsaw to leave their homes and walk to their deaths – these conquering beings, so confident of their own might when it had been a matter of slaughtering millions of women and children, turned out to be despicable, cringing reptiles as soon as it came to a life-and-death struggle. They begged for mercy. They lost their heads. They ran this way and that way like rats. They forgot about Treblinka's diabolically contrived defence system. They forgot about their all-annihilating fire-power. They forgot their own weapons. But need I say more? Need anyone be in the least surprised by these things?

Two and a half months later, on 14 October, 1943, there was an uprising in the Sobibór death factory; it was organized by a Soviet prisoner of war, a political commissar from Rostov by the name of Sashko Pechersky. The same thing happened as in Treblinka: people half dead from hunger managed to get the better of several hundred S.S. beasts who were bloated from the blood of the innocent. With the help of crude axes that they themselves had forged in the camp smithies, the rebels overpowered their execu-tioners. Many of the rebels had no weapon except sand. Pechersky had told them to fill their pockets with fine sand and throw it in the guards' eyes. But need we be surprised by any of this?

As Treblinka blazed and the rebels, saying a silent farewell to the ashes of their fellows, were escaping through the barbed wire, S.S. and police units were rushed in from all directions to track them down. Hundreds of police dogs were sent after them. Aeroplanes were summoned. There was fighting in the forests, fighting in the marshes – and few of those who took part in the uprising are still alive. But what does that matter? They died fighting, with guns in their hands.

After 2 August Treblinka ceased to exist. The Germans burned the remaining corpses, dismantled the stone buildings, removed the barbed wire and torched the wooden barracks not already burned down by the rebels. Part of the equipment of the house of death was blown up; part was taken away by train. The grills were destroyed, the excavators taken away, the vast pits filled in with earth. The station building was razed; last of all, the track was dismantled and the sleepers removed. Lupins were sown on the site of the camp, and a settler by the name of Streben built himself a little house there. Now this house has gone; it too was burned down. What were the Germans trying to do? To hide the traces of the murder of millions of people in the Hell that was Treblinka? Did they really imagine this to be possible? Can silence be imposed on thousands of people who have witnessed transports bringing the condemned from every corner of Europe to a place of conveyor-belt execution? Did the Germans really think that they could hide the dead, heavy flames and the smoke that stood in the sky for eight months, visible day and night to the inhabitants of dozens of villages and hamlets? Did they really think that they could force the peasants of Wólka to forget the screams of the women and children – those terrible screams that continued for thirteen months and that ring in their ears to this day? Can the memory of such screams be torn from the heart? Did they really think they could force silence upon the peasants who for a whole year had been transporting human ash from the camp and scattering it on to the roads round about?

Did they really think they could silence the still-living witnesses who had seen the Treblinka executioner's block in operation from its first days until 2 August, 1943, the last day of its existence? Witnesses whose descriptions of each S.S. man and each of the *Wachmänner* precisely corroborate one another? Witnesses whose step-by-step, hour-by-hour accounts of life in Treblinka have made it possible to create a kind of Treblinka diary? It is no longer possible to shout "*Mützen ab!*" at these witnesses; it is no longer possible to lead them into a gas chamber. And Himmler no longer has any power over his minions. Their heads bowed, their trembling fingers tugging nervously at the hems of their jackets, their voices dull and expressionless, Himmler's minions are now telling the story of their crimes – a story so unreal that it seems like the product of insanity and delirium. A Soviet officer, wearing the green ribbon of the Defence of Stalingrad medal, takes down page after page of the murderers' testimonies. At the door stands a sentry, wearing the same green Stalingrad ribbon on his chest. His lips are pressed tight together and there is a stern look on his gaunt weather-beaten face. This face is the face of justice – the people's justice. And is it not a remarkable symbol that one of the victorious armies from Stalingrad should have come to Treblinka, near Warsaw? It was not without reason that Himmler began to panic in February 1943; it was not without reason that he flew to Treblinka and gave orders for the construction of the grill pits followed by the obliteration of all traces of the camp. It was not without reason – but it was to no avail. The defenders of Stalingrad have now reached Treblinka; from the Volga to the Vistula turned out to be no distance at all. And now the very earth of Treblinka refuses to be an accomplice to the crimes the monsters committed. It is casting up the bones and belongings of those who were murdered; it is casting up everything that Hitler's people tried to bury within it.

———

We arrived in Treblinka in early September 1944, thirteen months after the day of the uprising. For thirteen months from July 1942 the executioner's block had been at work – and for thirteen months from August 1943, the Germans had been trying to obliterate every trace of this work.

It is quiet. The tops of the pine trees on either side of the railway line are barely stirring. It is these pines, this sand, this old tree stump that millions of human eyes saw as their freight wagons came slowly up to the platform. With true German neatness, whitewashed stones have been laid along the borders of the black road. The ashes and crushed cinders swish softly. We enter the camp. We tread the earth of Treblinka. The lupin pods split open at the least touch; they split with a faint ping and millions of tiny peas scatter over the earth. The sounds of the falling peas and the bursting pods come together to form a single soft, sad melody. It is as if a funeral knell – a barely audible, sad, broad, peaceful tolling – is being carried to us from the very depths of the earth. And, rich and swollen as if saturated with flax oil, the earth sways beneath our feet – earth of Treblinka, bottomless earth, earth as unsteady as the sea. This wilderness behind a barbed-wire fence has swallowed more human lives than all the earth's oceans and seas have swallowed since the birth of mankind.

The earth is casting up fragments of bone, teeth, sheets of paper, clothes, things of all kinds. The earth does not want to keep secrets.

And from the earth's unhealing wounds, from this earth that is splitting apart, things are escaping of their own accord. Here they are: the half-rotted shirts of those who were murdered, their trousers and shoes, their cigarette cases that have turned green, along with little cog-wheels from watches, pen-knives, shaving brushes, candlesticks, a child's shoes with red pompoms, embroidered towels from the Ukraine, lace underwear, scissors, thimbles, corsets and bandages. Out of another fissure in the earth have escaped heaps of utensils: frying pans, aluminium mugs, cups, pots and pans of all sizes, jars, little dishes, children's plastic mugs. In yet another place – as if all that the Germans had buried was being pushed up out of the swollen, bottomless earth, as if someone's hand were pushing it all out into the light of day: half-rotted Soviet passports, notebooks with Bulgarian writing, photographs of children from Warsaw and Vienna, letters pencilled in a childish scrawl, a small volume of poetry, a yellowed sheet of paper on which someone had copied a prayer, ration cards from Germany . . . And everywhere there are hundreds of perfume bottles of all shapes and sizes – green, pink, blue . . . And over all this reigns a terrible smell of decay, a smell that neither fire, nor sun, nor rain, nor snow, nor wind have been able to overcome. And thousands of little forest flies are crawling about over all these half-rotted bits and pieces, over all these papers and photographs.

We walk on over the swaying, bottomless earth of Treblinka and suddenly come to a stop. Thick wavy hair, gleaming like burnished copper, the delicate lovely hair of a young woman, trampled into the ground; and beside it, some equally fine blonde hair; and then some heavy black plaits on the bright sand; and then, more and more. . . Evidently these are the contents of a sack, just a single sack that somehow got left behind. Yes, it is all true. The last hope, the last wild hope that it was all just a terrible dream, has gone. And the lupin pods keep popping open, and the tiny peas keep pattering down – and this really does all sound like a funeral knell rung by countless little bells from under the earth. And it feels as if your heart must come to a stop now, gripped by more sorrow, more grief, more anguish than any human being can endure. . .

Scholars, sociologists, criminologists, psychiatrists and philosophers – everyone is asking how all this can have happened. How indeed? Was it something organic? Was it a matter of heredity, upbringing, environment or external conditions? Was it a matter of historical fate, or the criminality of the German leaders? Somehow the embryonic traits of a racial theory that sounded simply comic when expounded by the second-rate charlatan professors or pathetic provincial theoreticians of nineteenth-century Germany – the contempt in which the German philistine held "Russian pigs", "Polish cattle", "Jews reeking of garlic", "debauched Frenchmen", "English shopkeepers", "hypocritical Greeks" and "Czech blockheads"; all the nonsense about the superiority of the Germans to every other race on earth, all the cheap nonsense that seemed so comical, such an easy target for journalists and humorists – all this, in the course of only a few years, ceased to seem merely infantile and was transformed into a threat to mankind. It became a deadly threat to human life and freedom and a source of unparalleled crime, bloodshed and suffering. There is much now to think about, much that we must try to understand.

Wars like the present war are terrible indeed. A vast amount of innocent blood has been spilt by the Germans. But it is not enough now to speak about Germany's responsibility for what has happened. Today we need to speak about the responsibility of every nation in the world; we need to speak about the responsibility of every nation and every citizen for the future.

Every man and woman today is duty-bound to his or her conscience, to his or her son and to his or her mother, to their motherland and to humanity as a whole to devote all the powers of their heart and mind to answering these questions: what is it that has given birth to racism? What can be done to prevent Nazism from ever rising again, either on this side or on the far side of the ocean? What can be done to make sure that Hitlerism is never, never in all eternity, resurrected?

What led Hitler and his followers to construct Majdanek, Sobibór, Bełżec, Auschwitz and Treblinka is the imperialist idea of exceptionalism – of racial, national and every other kind of exceptionalism.

We must remember that Fascism and racism will emerge from this war not only with the bitterness of defeat but also with sweet memories of the ease with which it is possible to commit mass murder. It has turned out that it is really not so very difficult to kill entire nations. Ten small chambers – hardly enough space, if properly furnished, to stable a hundred horses – ten such chambers turned out to be enough to kill three million people.

Killing turned out to be supremely easy – it does not entail any uncommon expenditure.

It is possible to build five hundred such chambers in only a few days. This is no more difficult than constructing a five-storey building.

It is possible to demonstrate with nothing more than a pencil that any large construction company with experience in the use of reinforced concrete can, in the course of six months and with a properly organized labour force, construct more than enough chambers to gas the entire population of the earth.

This must be unflinchingly borne in mind by everyone who truly values honour, freedom and the life of all nations, the life of humanity.

Translated from the Russian by Robert Chandler

FURTHER READING

Treblinka: testimony and reportage

Richard Glazar, *Trap with a Green Fence: Survival in Treblinka*, trans. Roslyn Theobald (Evanston: Northwestern University Press, 1995)

Vasily Grossman, *The Road: Short Fiction and Essays*, trans. Robert and Elizabeth Chandler with Olga Mukovnikova (London: MacLehose Press, 2010)

Vasily Grossman, *A Writer at War*, ed. and trans. Antony Beevor and Luba Vinogradova (London: Pimlico, 2005)

Claude Lanzmann, *Shoah: An Oral History of the Holocaust* (New York: Pantheon, 1985)

Gitta Sereny, *Into that Darkness: From Mercy Killing to Mass Murder* (London: André Deutsch, 1974; reissued Pimlico, 1995)

Yankel Wiernik, *A Year in Treblinka: An Inmate Who Escaped Tells the Day-to-Day Facts of His Tortuous Experience* (New York: American Representation of the General Jewish Workers' Union of Poland, 1945)

Samuel Willenberg, *Surviving Treblinka*, trans. Naftali Greenwood (London: Basil Blackwell, 1989)

Histories of the Final Solution and Operation Reinhard

Yitzhak Arad, *Belzec, Sobibor, Treblinka: The Operation Reinhard Death Camps* (Bloomington: Indiana University Press, 1987)

Saul Friedländer, *Nazi Germany and the Jews*, 2 vols (New York: HarperCollins, 1997, 2007)

Raul Hilberg, *The Destruction of the European Jews*, third ed., 3 vols (New Haven: Yale University Press, 2003)